The Best 5
of Sherlock Holmes
by Sherlockian

英語で読むシャーロック・ホームズ

シャーロキアンが愛した5篇

コナン・ドイル
原著

井上久美
翻訳・英語解説

ナレーター

Jack Merluzzi
Chris Koprowski

●

イラスト

Tomoko Taguchi

シャーロック・ホームズって誰？

大村数一（エディター）

　シャーロキアン（Sherlockian）という「おかしな」人たちがいる。クリスチャン（Christian）がキリストを信じているように、この人たちはシャーロック・ホームズが実在の人物だと信じているのだ。そしてクリスチャンにとっては聖書がすべてであるように、シャーロキアンにとっては60編（長編4、短編56）のホームズ物語が「聖書」であり、ここに書かれていることはすべて真実だと信じている。

　「ふつうの」人は、このホームズの冒険談を書いたのはイギリスの作家、アーサー・コナン・ドイル（1859-1930）だと思っているが、シャーロキアンに言わせれば、「とんでもない」間違いである。読めば分かるとおり、書いたのはホームズの友人で医師のジョン・ワトソン、ドイルはワトソンの原稿を出版社に売り込んだ版権代理人にすぎないのだ。シャーロキアンたちは日夜この「聖書」を読み、ホームズの実像をさぐっている。そんな彼らの研究成果をもとに、ホームズとはどんな人物なのか紹介してみよう。

　ホームズは1854年1月6日にヨークシャーで生まれた。大学はオックスフォードに入学し、ケンブリッジに転校したと考えられるが、両大学には彼の在学を証明するものがなく探索が続いている。1877年にロンドンで私立探偵を開業、1881年にはワトソン医師と共同でベーカー街221Bに間借りし、探偵事務所にした。このときからワトソンによるホームズの活躍記録がはじまり、名声が高まっていく。

　記録のなかでいちばん古いものは、1874年、大学時代に同級生の家に起こった事件を解決して、探偵を職業とするきっかけになったものであ

り、いちばん新しいものは1914年、ドイツのスパイ網をあばく仕事だった。このときはもう引退して養蜂を楽しんでいたが、イギリス首相のたっての依頼で引き受けたのだ。

　このベーカー街221Bがシャーロキアンにとっては「聖地」である。この部屋でホームズは数々の推理をし、化学の実験をしてワトソンを悩ませ、ヴァイオリン（なんとストラディバリウスの名器を持っていた）を奏で、事件がないときには退屈のあまりコカイン（このころは違法なものではなかった）を注射していた。

　ホームズは180センチの長身、薄く高い鼻と鋭い灰色の眼が印象的である。探偵としては護身術が不可欠だが、ホームズは腕力にすぐれ、フェンシング、棒術、ボクシングの達人であり、日本の武術「バリツ」も身につけている。もちろん変装の巧みさはいろいろな場面で発揮しているし、犯罪捜査に必要な心理学、毒物学、解剖学などに精通していた。

　……さて今日のベーカー街では、どんな事件が起こっているのだろう。

本書の構成

　本書は、

　　□ 英語本文に対応する日本語訳　　　□ 欄外の語注
　　□ ストーリー毎のフレーズ解説　　　□ MP3形式の英文を収録した音声

で構成されています。本書は、ホームズの短篇の英文抄訳と日本語訳を読み進めることで、そのストーリーを楽しみながら、同時に受験やビジネスシーンなどでも役に立つ英語フレーズも習得できるようになっています。

　ストーリーの区切りごとのQRコードをスマートフォンで読み取ると、該当部分の英語音声を聞くことができます。繰り返して聞いていただくことで、発音のチェックだけでなく、英語で物語を理解する力がさらに深まります。

＊本書は左ページに英語、右ページに日本語を配し、対照して読み進めていただけるようつくられています。必ずしも同じ位置から始めることは難しいのですが、なるべく該当の日本語が見つけられやすいように、ところどころ行をあけるなどして調整してあります。

目次

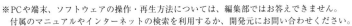

A SCANDAL

ボヘミア国王がベーカー街のホームズの部屋を訪ねてきた。
ある国の王女と結婚するにあたり、昔つきあっていた女性といっしょに
撮った写真をとりもどしてほしいというのだ……

この最初の短編が1891年、月刊誌『ストランド』に掲載されるや
大評判になる。この後『赤毛組合』『まだらの紐』などの名作が
毎号連載され、5万部だったこの雑誌の発行部数が
あっというまに50万部になってしまった。

女嫌いのホームズがただひとり「あの女性」と呼ぶ
アイリーン・アドラーが登場し、この名探偵と頭脳勝負をくりひろげる
というファンにとっては「たまらない」作品。
ホームズがアイリーンに恋愛感情をもっていたかどうかについては
論争が続いているが、シャーロキアンたちの「永遠のマドンナ」
であることは確かである。

ちなみに国王が当座の費用にとしてホームズに渡した1000ポンドは
現在の価値に換算すると2400万円に相当する。

IN BOHEMIA

ボヘミアの醜聞

A Scandal in Bohemia

To Sherlock Holmes, she is always *the* woman. I have seldom heard him call her anything else. In his eyes she represents the very best of all women. It was not that Holmes loved the late Irene Adler. He did not allow himself to feel any emotion, particularly love for a woman. He kept his mind cold and exact and very balanced. In my opinion Sherlock Holmes was the most perfect mind that the world has ever seen. But he never spoke of the softer feelings, except with sarcasm. He would not let himself feel a strong emotion; it would upset him too much. But there was one woman for him, and that woman was Irene Adler, someone remembered by perhaps nobody else.

■ the 冠 極めつけの ■ seldom 副 滅多に～しない ■ represent 動 象徴する、意味する ■ very best 最高の ■ late 形 故～ ■ emotion 形 感情 ■ particularly 副 特別に、とりわけ ■ exact 形 正確な、精密な ■ In my opinion 私の考えでは、私見では ■ speak of ～を口にする ■ sarcasm 名 皮肉 ■ upset 動 動揺させる

ボヘミアの醜聞

　シャーロック・ホームズにとって、彼女はいつも「あの女性（ひと）」だった。ほかの呼び方をするのを聞いたことはめったにない。彼の目には、彼女はこの世で最高の女性に映っているのだ。とはいっても、ホームズが故アイリーン・アドラーに恋していたわけではない。彼は、何らかの感情、ましてや恋愛感情を抱くことを拒絶していた。いつも冷静で緻密、均衡のとれた精神状態に保っていた。私のみたところでは、シャーロック・ホームズは、この世で最も完璧な精神をもつ人間である。しかし、彼が皮肉を交えずに、人の微妙な気持ちについて語ることはなかった。強い感情というものをあえてもたないようにしている。気持ちが乱されるからだ。しかし、ホームズにも、ひとりの女性がいた。そして、その女性がアイリーン・アドラー。彼女のことを憶えている人はおそらく彼以外にはいない。

Holmes and I had not met for a long time. I had married and now spent a lot of time with my wife in complete happiness. Our new home kept me busy. Holmes, by contrast, kept away from people as far as possible, living at our old apartment on Baker Street, reading his thousands of books and making plans with his fiery mind. As in the old days, he studied crime, trying to help solve mysteries which the police had given up trying to understand. From time to time, I heard about him helping the police to solve a mystery of this sort. The last time he had helped the ruling family of Holland solve one of these problems. But I only learned through the newspaper, and I shared this information with all the other thousands of readers of the British papers. It had been a long time since I had met my friend and talked with him.

One night, it was March 20, 1888, I was passing Baker Street on my way from a patient's home. How I missed my friend. I wondered what case he was working on now. As I looked in the window, I saw his tall body. I knew the way he was walking, holding his hands behind his back. I rang the bell, and he opened the door to let me into the rooms I had shared with him before my marriage.

■ by contrast それに反して　■ keep away from ～から離れている、～に近づかない
■ fiery 形 炎のような　■ crime 名 犯罪　■ solve 動 解決する　■ from time to time 時々　■ ruling family 王族　■ Holland 名 オランダ　■ share 動 共有する
■ paper 名 新聞　■ on one's way from ～から帰る途中で　■ miss 動 ～いないのを寂しく思う　■ case 名 事件

　ホームズと私は、長い間会っていなかった。私は結婚し、今では生活の大半を伴侶とともに、このうえなく幸せに暮らしていた。家庭をもったことで私は忙しくなったが、ホームズの方は、可能な限り世の中に背を向け、かつて私と暮らしていたベーカー街の下宿で、本を読みふけり、精力的に何かしら考えを練ったりして暮らしていた。かつてのように、犯罪を研究し、警察があきらめた事件の解決に乗り出していた。時折、彼が警察に協力してその種の事件を解いたという噂を耳にした。最近のものでは、オランダ王室が関わる事件に協力したというものもあった。しかし、私はただ新聞を通して知るだけ、全国紙の一読者として情報を得ているにすぎなかった。ホームズと会って、会話を交わしていたころから、長い時間がたっていた。

　ある夜——それは1888年3月20日のことだった——私は患者の往診から帰る途中、ベーカー街を通りかかった。友に会いたくなった。今、どんな事件に取り組んでいるのだろう。彼の家の窓を見ると、背の高い人影が映った。手を後ろに組んで歩く様子は憶えがある。呼び鈴を鳴らすと、ホームズは扉を開け、部屋に招き入れてくれた。結婚する前は私も一緒に暮らしていた部屋だ。

He did not say anything, but he seemed glad to see me. With a kindly look, he waved me to an armchair. After I had sat down, he stood in front of the fire, and looked at me very carefully. Then he said, "I think you have gained seven and a half pounds since I last saw you."

"Seven," I answered.

"A little more, I think," Holmes continued. "And you did not tell me that you were going to work as a doctor again. Finally, it appears your servant girl is very careless."

"Holmes! How do you know all these things? If you had lived several hundred years ago, they would have burned you as a witch. It is true that I went for a long country walk and got caught in the rain last week, but I am wearing different clothes today. How can you say that my servant is careless?"

"Well," Holmes replied with a smile on his lips, "I see your shoe has been scraped carelessly. There are many cuts on it as though someone was trying to remove mud. As for your working again as a doctor, well, I smell strong chemicals on your hands and I see the bump under your hat of the stethoscope which you carry there."

■ armchair 图 肘掛け椅子　■ gain 動 ～を増す、加える　■ pound ポンド《重量の単位。約453.6g》　■ appear 動 ～のように見える、～と思われる　■ servant 图 使用人　■ If S had p.p., S' would have p.p.（昔）～だったら（昔）…だったろう《仮定法過去完了》　■ witch 图 魔女　■ get caught 捕らえられる　■ reply 動 返答する、答える

　彼は何も言わなかったが、私との再会を喜んでいるようだった。温かいまなざしで、肘掛け椅子に座るように手で促した。私が腰かけると、彼は暖炉の前に立ち、私をじっくりと観察した。そして口を開くと、「最後に会った時から7.5ポンド増えたようだな」と言った。

　「7ポンドだ」と私は答えた。
　「もう少しあると思うがね」とホームズが続ける。「医者に復帰したことを僕には黙っていたね。それに、君の雇っているメイドはひどく気が利かないようだ」
　「ホームズ！　いったいどうしてそれを？　君、数百年前に生きていたら、魔女扱いされて火あぶりの刑になっているぞ。たしかに先週、田舎道を延々と歩いていて雨にふられたんだ。でも、今日は別の服を着ているよ。どうしてメイドが気が利かないとわかった？」

　「ふふん」とホームズは口元に笑みを浮かべた。「君の靴に、ぞんざいに擦った痕がある。泥を取り除こうとして、あちこち傷つけてしまったんだろう。医師に復帰したことについては、君の手から強い薬品の匂いがしたし、帽子がいやに膨らんでいるからね。聴診器が入っているんだろう？」

■ scrape 動 ゴシゴシこする　■ cut 名 切れ目、傷口　■ as though まるで〜であるかのように　■ mud 名 泥　■ as for 〜に関しては　■ chemical 名 化学薬品　■ bump 名 突起、隆起　■ stethoscope 名 聴診器

I could only laugh when he explained how easy it was for him to understand my recent past. "When you give your reasons, the thing always appears so simple, I feel silly. I wonder how you see so many things. My eyes are just as good, but I can't see them until you explain them."

"The problem, Watson, is that you do not pay attention," Holmes kindly explained. "For example, you have seen the hall steps that lead to this room?"

"Of course I have."

"How many times?"

"Well, hundreds."

"Then, how many steps are there?"

"How many? I've never counted them."

"Quite so. You have not observed. And yet you have seen. That is just my point. Now, I know that there are seventeen steps because I have both seen and observed."

Holmes continued, "By the way, have a look at this letter I received today." It told Holmes that he would have a visitor at eight o'clock that night and that he must not miss his visitor. The note sounded very important.

■ recent 形 最近の ■ silly 形 愚かな ■ pay attention 注意を払う ■ quite so そうだろうとも ■ observe 動 観察する ■ and yet それにもかかわらず ■ by the way ところで ■ have a look at ～を見る

　私の近況をたやすく推理した様子を説明され、私は笑うしかなかった。「君の推理を聴くと、いつだってあまりにも簡単に思えて、自分がなんて愚かなんだろうと思うよ。どうやったらそんなにたくさんのことが見えるんだい。私の目も負けてはいないんだよ。でも、君に説明してもらうまで、何も見えないんだよ」

　「ワトソン君、問題はね、君が注意を向けていないということだよ」と、ホームズは親切に教えてくれた。「例えば、この部屋に上る階段を見てきたよね」

　「もちろんさ」
　「何回ぐらい?」
　「そうだな、何百回も」
　「それなら、何段あるかな?」
　「何段?　そんなの数えたことないな」
　「そうだろうとも。君は観察していないんだ。でも見てはいる。それが僕の言いたかったことだ。さあ。僕は17段あると知っているよ。だって、見て、観察しているからね」

　ホームズは続けた。「ところで、この手紙を見てくれ。今日届いたんだ」。その手紙には、今夜8時に客が尋ねてくるので、家にいて欲しいとの旨が書かれていた。非常に深刻な様子が感じられた。

The paper was very thick. Holmes told me to hold it up to the light and I saw the letters "Eg P Gt" but I did not know what they meant. Holmes continued, " 'Gt' is a standard way of referring to business in German. 'P' of course stands for paper. The 'Eg,' well, looking at the map of Germany, I see the town Egria. So what do you make of that?"

I replied slowly, "That the paper is made in Germany."

"Quite. And the man who wrote it is German."

It was just eight o'clock and we heard horses coming down the street. I tried to leave, but Holmes pushed me gently into a chair and asked me to watch carefully.

The man who entered was very, very tall. He looked like Hercules and was wearing a dark blue coat with a red scarf at the neck. His boots were lined in thick brown fur and he carried a hat in his hand. We could not see his face because he was wearing a mask.

"Did you receive my note?" he asked with a heavy German accent.

"Please sit down," Holmes replied.

The man began to tell his story.

■ thick 形 厚い　■ hold ～ up to the light ～を持ち上げ光に透かす　■ refer to ～に言及する　■ stand for ～を表す　■ Egria 名 エグリア《地名》　■ enter 動 ～に入る　■ Hercules 名 ヘラクレス　■ line 動 ～に裏地を付ける、～の内側を覆う　■ fur 名 毛皮　■ accent 名 訛り

　厚手の便箋だった。ホームズがその紙を光に透かしてみるように言うので見てみると、「Eg P Gt」という文字が入っているのがわかった。しかし、私にはその意味するところはわからなかった。ホームズが続けた。「Gt」はドイツ語で会社を意味する標準的な書き方だ。Pはもちろん紙のこと。「Eg」は、そう、ドイツの地図を見ると、エグリア（Egria）という地名があるね。これは何を意味すると思う?」

　「この紙はドイツで作られたということか」と私はおずおずと答えた。

　「その通り。そして、これを書いた男はドイツ人だということだ」

　ちょうど8時、通りを駆ける馬の蹄の音が聞こえた。私は帰ろうとしたが、ホームズが私をやさしく椅子に押し戻し、ここで気をつけて観察してくれと言った。

　入ってきた男は並外れて背丈が高く、ヘラクレスを思わせる様相で、群青色のコートを着て、首には赤いスカーフを巻いていた。ブーツの上部には茶色の毛皮がたっぷりとあしらわれ、帽子を手にしていた。顔は見えなかった。仮面を付けていたからだ。

　「手紙は届きましたか」と、彼は強いドイツ語なまりで聞いてきた。

　「おかけください」とホームズが答えた。
　男は語り始めた。

"You must not tell anyone about what I am about to say. I have a small problem, but if it is told to a newspaper, it could cause great embarrassment to one of the most important families in Europe."

Holmes and I both nodded our heads in understanding. Then Holmes sat down and after closing his eyes, said, "If you do not tell me the problem, though, I cannot help you."

At this the man jumped up and tore off his mask saying, "All right! I am the King. I will not hide it."

"Why, indeed?" Holmes asked. "As soon as you entered this room I knew that you were your Majesty, Wilhelm Gottsreich Sigismond von Ormstein, Grand Duke and the future king of Germany."

Hearing this, our visitor sat down and spoke quietly. "But I am not used to speaking to people directly. I came from Prague to talk to you because I cannot trust anyone else with this matter."

"Please tell me," Holmes said, again closing his eyes.

"Yes, the facts are very short. Five years ago I met an opera singer named Irene Adler from New Jersey while she was singing in Warsaw. I wrote her some letters expressing my feelings, and now I would like to have those letters back again."

"Why are you so worried about a few letters?" Holmes asked.

■ be about to まさに〜しようとしている ■ cause 動 〜を引き起こす ■ embarrassment 名 困惑 ■ nod 動 うなずく ■ tear off はぎ取る ■ hide 動 隠す ■ Why, indeed?「一体、どうして？」 ■ Majesty 名 陛下 ■ Grand Duke 大公 ■ be used to 〜に慣れている ■ Prague 名 プラハ《チェコ共和国の首都》 ■ trust 動 信用する ■ matter 名 事柄、問題 ■ Warsaw 名 ワルシャワ《ポーランドの首都》

18

「私がこれから申し上げることは、決して他言されないように。今ちょっとした問題を抱えている。ちょっとしたとはいっても、この情報が新聞などに漏れてしまえば、ヨーロッパでも有数の名家に多大な辱めがもたらされることになる」

ホームズと私は、同意の記しに深くうなずいた。それからホームズは、椅子にもたれると目を閉じていった。「しかし、その問題を包み隠さずお話ししていただかないことには、お助けすることはできませんよ」

これを聞いて男は跳び上がり、仮面をはぎ取って言った。「いかにも、余は王である。隠すつもりはない」

「なぜわかったのか?」とホームズ。「この部屋に入っていらしたとたんにわかりました。ヴィルヘルム・ゴッツライヒ・ジギスモント・フォン・オルムシュタイン大公(ボヘミア国王)、後にドイツ国王になられる方だということが」

これを聞くと客は椅子に腰を下ろし、静かに語り始めた。「私が直々に人に相談するなど異例のことだ。プラハから貴殿を訪ねてきたのは、この件についてほかに信頼できる人物がいないからだ」

ホームズは「どうぞ、お話し下さい」と促すと、再び目を閉じた。

「そう複雑な話ではないのだ。5年前、私はワルシャワでアイリーン・アドラーというオペラ歌手と出会った。ニュー・ジャージー州生まれの歌手で、ワルシャワで活動していた。私は彼女に何通か手紙を書き、思いを伝えた。だが今はその手紙を取り返したい」

「ほんの何通かの手紙をなぜそれほど心配なさるのですか?」とホームズは聞いた。

"It is the photograph of both of us which I sent her that I most want back."

"Oh, that was foolish," Holmes advised him.

"Yes," the prince replied, "it was. I was insane. And very young. I am thirty now. And I am about to be married to the second daughter of the King of Scandinavia. If she heard anything about this Adler affair, I would have no chance of marrying the woman of my dreams in Scandinavia."

"Are you sure she would try to ruin your chances of happiness with another woman?"

"Yes, she has promised to send the picture on the day of my formal engagement, which is next Monday."

"So, we have three days," said Holmes with a yawn. "Leave me your hotel number so that I can contact you. And what about money?"

"There is no limit. I would give you part of my country to save my name. For the moment, I'll give you three hundred pounds in gold and seven hundred in notes," he said, laying the money on the table.

Holmes got the address for Irene Adler and asked me to come back at three o'clock the following day to chat about the matter.

■ foolish 形 愚かな ■ insane 形 正気でない ■ affair 名 出来事、スキャンダル ■ ruin 動 ～を台無しにする ■ yawn 名 あくび ■ so that ～できるように ■ contact 動 連絡を取る ■ save one's name 自分の名誉を保つ ■ for the moment 差し当たり ■ pound 名 ポンド《イギリスの貨幣単位》 ■ note 名 紙幣 ■ lay 動 ～を置く ■ chat about ～を雑談する

「私が一番取り戻したいのは、ふたりで撮った写真なのだ」

「なんと、それは軽率でしたね」とホームズは言った。
「そのとおりだ。私はどうかしていた。若気の至りだ。今は30になり、スカンジナヴィア国王の第二王女との結婚を控えている。アドラーのことが王女の耳に少しでも入ったら、この結婚など夢のまた夢になってしまう」

「アドラー嬢が、あなたが別の女性と結婚するのを邪魔しようとしているのは確かですか?」
「間違いない。彼女は結婚の公式発表の日、つまり来週の月曜日に写真を送ると約束してきた」
「では、3日間の猶予がありますね」とホームズはあくびをしながら言った。「私から連絡がとれるよう、ご滞在のホテルの番号を教えていただけますか。それから報酬の方は?」
「いかようにも。私の名誉が守られるのならば、王国の一部を与えてもよい。当面の費用として、金貨300ポンド、紙幣700ポンドを置いておこう」と王は言い、テーブルの上に置いた。

ホームズはアイリーン・アドラーの住所を書き留めると、私に、この件について話し合いたいから、翌日の3時にまた来てくれと言った。

2

At three o'clock the next day, I was at his room, but he was nowhere to be seen. The maid told me that he had not returned since morning when he left around eight a.m. I decided to wait for him, no matter how long, and sat down. It was always such a pleasure to study his system of work. His reasoning was so fast. He had such quick and subtle methods of solving mysteries. He never failed, either.

About an hour had passed quietly when, suddenly, he came in, looking very tired. He disappeared into the bedroom for five minutes. When he came back in the sitting room, he looked fresh and relaxed. Then he sat down, laughing.

"You cannot imagine how I passed my morning."

"I suppose you were watching Miss Adler."

■ maid 图 メイド ■ no matter how どんなに～であろうとも ■ system 图 流儀、方式 ■ reasoning 图 推理 ■ subtle 形 微妙な、繊細な ■ fail 動 失敗する ■ come in 入って来る ■ disappear into ～に姿を消す ■ sitting room 居間、リビングルーム ■ pass 動（時を）過ごす

2

　翌日の3時、私はホームズの部屋に行ったが、彼の姿はどこにも見えなかった。メイドによれば、彼は朝8時に家を出てから戻ってきていないという。私は、どれだけ遅くなっても彼を待とうと決め、腰を下ろした。ホームズの仕事の方法を研究するのは、いつだって楽しい。その推理の迅速なこと。彼は絶妙な方法で瞬時に謎を解く術を心得ていた。そして、失敗することもなかった。

　1時間ほどが静かに過ぎ、突然、彼が入ってきた。ひどく疲れているようだった。寝室に引っ込んだが、5分ほどして居間に戻ってきたときには、すっきりとリラックスしているようだった。それから彼は笑いながら腰を下ろした。

「僕が今朝、何をしてきたか、君には想像できないだろうね」
「アドラー嬢を偵察にいったんだろう」

"Yes. But it was still a very unusual morning. I found her house. The sitting room has long windows almost to the floor. They can be easily opened by a child from outside. I walked around the house and examined it carefully. Nothing unusual. Down the road I found a mews and the horsekeepers. I helped them clean their horses, and they told me all about the people in the neighborhood. Most of their talk was very boring, but at least I could learn a lot about Miss Adler, too."

"What about her?" I asked.

"She has turned all the men's heads in the town. She is beautiful, lives quietly, sings at concerts, drives at five every day and returns for dinner at seven. She has only one male visitor—a lawyer named Mr. Godfrey Norton. He comes once, sometimes twice a day. He is very handsome and young.

"After I listened to the horsekeepers' talk, I walked around those streets for a while. Who was this Mr. Godfrey Norton? If she hired him to protect her from the king, maybe she had given him the photograph. But if he is her lover, then she wouldn't give him the photograph.

■ unusual 形 普通でない ■ examine 動 調べる ■ mews 名 うまや ■ horsekeeper 名 馬丁 ■ neighborhood 名 近所 ■ boring 形 退屈な、つまらない ■ at least 少なくとも ■ turn someone's head （人）を振り向かせる ■ male 名 男性 ■ handsome 形 ハンサムな ■ for a while しばらく（の間） ■ hire 動 雇う ■ lover 名 恋人

「その通り。でも、そうそうない体験だよ。彼女の家を見つけた。居間には床に届くほどの大きな窓があった。子供でも外から簡単に開けられるような窓だったよ。家のまわりを歩いて仔細に観察してみたが、特に目立ったところはなかった。通りを歩いてみると、厩舎があって、馬番がいた。馬にブラシをかけるのを手伝ってやったら、近所の人たちの噂をあれこれ話してくれた。大半はつまらない話だったけれども、少なくとも、アドラー嬢についてはかなりの情報を得ることができたよ」

「どんな女性なんだね?」
「町中の男性を虜にしているんだ。容姿端麗。暮らしぶりは静かで、コンサートで歌い、毎日5時に出かけ、7時に夕食に帰ってくる。出入りのある男の客はひとりだけ。ゴドフリー・ノートンという弁護士だ。1日1度、時には2度やってくる。男前な若者らしい。

馬番の話を聴いたあと、しばらくあたりの道を歩き回った。ゴドフリー・ノートンとは何者か? アイリーンが王から身を守るために彼を雇ったのならば、写真を彼に渡しているだろう。でも、恋人だったら、写真を渡しているとは考えにくい。

"As I was walking, a cab drove up to her house. A gentleman of the horsekeepers' description jumped out. He was in the house for about half an hour. I could see him talking and waving his arms. I couldn't see Miss Adler. Then he jumped into the cab and shouted, 'To the Church of St. Monica's.'

"I was trying to get a cab to follow him, when she came running out of the house and jumped into her cab. She was a lovely woman, with a face that a man might die for.

"'Hurry to the Church of St. Monica,' she called out to her driver.

"A cab passed at that moment and I jumped into it, calling out, 'The Church of St. Monica, as fast as you can go.'

"My cabby drove fast, faster than I had ever gone in my life, I think. But when we reached the church, the two other cabs were standing empty with steaming horses in front of the door. I walked into the back of the church quietly, as though I was just an ordinary sightseer. Suddenly, to my surprise, Godfrey Norton came running as hard as he could toward me.

"'Thank God,' he cried. 'You'll do. Come! Come!'

"'What then?' I asked.

■ cab 图 馬車　■ drive up 車でやって来る　■ description 图 記述、描写　■ jump out 飛び出す　■ come running out of ～から走って出て来る　■ die for 非常に魅力的と感じる　■ call out 叫ぶ　■ cabby 图 御者　■ steaming 形 湯気を立てている　■ ordinary 形 普通の、どこにでもある　■ sightseer 图 観光客　■ Thank God.「神に感謝する」

　歩いていると、馬車が彼女の家の前に止まるのが見えた。馬番が言っていたとおりのいでたちの紳士が飛び降りた。彼は30分ほど彼女の家の中にいて、腕を振りながら話をしているのが見えた。アドラー嬢の姿は見えなかった。それから彼は馬車に飛び乗り、『セント・モニカ教会へ』と叫んだ。

　馬車をつかまえて後を追おうかと思っていたところへ、家から女が飛び出してきて、彼女の馬車に乗り込んだ。魅力的な女性だった。男が命を捧げるのもわかるような風貌だった。
　『セント・モニカ教会へ。急いで』と彼女は御者に言った。

　その瞬間、一台の馬車が通りかかった。僕は急いで飛び乗り、叫んだ。『セント・モニカ教会。できるだけ急いでくれ』
　馬車は速かった。あんなに速い馬車に乗るのは初めてだった。教会に着いたときには、前の2台の馬車の中は空っぽ。まだ息がはずんでいる馬と馬車だけが玄関前に停車していた。僕はごく普通の見物人のふりをして、教会の奥へと進んでいった。すると突然、ゴドフリー・ノートンが僕に向かって全速力で駆け寄ってきたんだ。驚いたよ。

　『ああ、神様、感謝します』と彼は言った。『君ならできる。来てくれ、さあ』
　『いったい何ですか』と聞いたが、

" 'Come, man, come, only three minutes, or it won't be legal.'

"He almost carried me to the altar where I repeated things I was told to say so that the man and woman standing there became man and wife. Thinking about me being the only person invited to their wedding is what made me burst out laughing just now.

"The minister told them they had to have a friend with them at the wedding or he couldn't marry them. That is why Mr. Norton was so upset. The bride gave me a gold coin after the ceremony.

"I thought they would leave together from the church and that I would have a lot of trouble getting the photograph. But he drove away alone and she went back to her home. 'I shall drive out in the park at five as usual,' she said as she left him. I heard no more. I drove off to make my own plans."

"Which are?" I asked.

"To have dinner and explain the work that you will do with me."

"I shall be delighted," I replied.

"I was sure that I could rely on you, Watson. We must be at Miss Adler's home when she returns from her drive in the park. There will be a small problem, and I will be carried into her house. You must promise not to help me. Only do as I instruct you. Remain close to the front window."

■legal 形 合法の　■altar 名 祭壇　■repeat 動 復唱する　■burst out laughing プッと噴き出す　■minister 名 牧師　■bride 名 花嫁　■ceremony 名 式典　■drive away 車で走り去る　■drive out 車で出掛ける　■drive off 車で走り去る　■delighted 形 喜んで　■rely 動 〜を頼りにする　■instruct 動 〜に指示する　■remain 動 (場所に)とどまる　■close to 〜の近くに

『来てくれ。さあ、こちらに。3分しかないんだ。でないと法的に認められなくなる』

彼は僕を引きずるようにして祭壇に連れて行き、僕は耳元でささやかれた言葉を復唱した。そこに立っている男女が夫婦となれるようにね。僕がふたりの結婚式に招かれた唯一の人間になったのかと思うとおかしくて、さっき思わず笑いがこみあげてきたんだ。

牧師は彼らに、立ち会い人がいないと結婚を認めないと言ったんだ。だからノートン氏は慌てていたんだよ。式の後で、花嫁は僕に金貨を一枚くれた。

彼らが教会からふたりで一緒に去ってしまったら、写真を取り戻すのが非常に難しくなると考えた。でも、男はひとりで馬車に乗り、女は自宅に戻った。『いつものように、5時に馬車で公園へ』と、彼女は別れ際に男に告げた。それ以上は聞こえなかった。僕は自分の手筈を整えるために戻ってきたんだ」

「手筈って?」

「夕食をとること。そして、君に、これから協力してほしい仕事の説明をすること」

「よろこんで」と僕は答えた。

「ワトソン君、僕は本当に君を頼りにしているんだ。アドラー嬢が公園から戻ってくるまでには、彼女の家に着いていなくてはならない。ちょっと面倒なことになるだろう。僕は彼女の家へ運ばれていくことになると思う。でも、手出しをしないと約束してくれ。僕が指示したことだけをしてほしいんだ。居間の窓の近くに待機していてくれ」

"I see."

"Watch me."

"Yes."

"And when I raise my hand, throw into the room what I give you to throw, and call out 'Fire!' Do you understand?"

"Completely."

Then he gave me a brown roll from his pocket.

"This is not dangerous. When you throw it into the room, it will catch fire. When you call out 'Fire,' many people will come running. You will leave the house and walk down to the street corner where I will meet you after ten minutes. Everything clear?"

"Yes."

"Excellent."

Again he disappeared into his bedroom, and when he came out after a few minutes he was changed completely. Now he was a friendly and simple-minded minister, dressed in a black hat with big trousers, a white tie, kindly smile and look. It was not only his clothes that Holmes changed. It was his entire being. His very soul seemed to change with the new part he took. He would have been a great actor on the stage, or a great scientist in the laboratory.

■ raise 動 ～を（持ち）上げる ■ throw 動 投げる ■ completely 副 完全に ■ roll 名 筒状のもの ■ dangerous 形 危険な ■ excellent 間 大変結構です ■ come out 出て くる ■ simple-minded 形 純真な ■ trousers 名 ズボン ■ tie 名 ネクタイ ■ entire 形 全体の ■ being 名 存在 ■ part 名 (配)役 ■ laboratory 名 研究室

30

「わかった」

「そして僕を見ていてくれ」

「ふむ」

「僕が手を挙げたら、これから渡すものを部屋の中に投げ込んでくれ。そして『火事だ』と叫ぶんだ。わかったかい?」

「了解」

それからホームズは、ポケットから茶色の筒を取り出して私に渡した。

「危険なものではないよ。部屋に投げ込んだら火が付くはずさ。『火事だ』と叫べば、大勢の人が駆けつける。君は家から離れて、通りの角まで歩いていってくれ。そこで10分後に会おう。わかったかい?」

「ああ」

「よし」

ホームズは再び寝室に姿を消した。そして数分後に出てきた時には、すっかり別人の姿——黒いつばひろ帽に幅広ズボン、白いネクタイといういでたちで、素朴で人のよさそうな笑顔の牧師——に変身していた。彼は全身で牧師を演じ、心もまた、新しい役になりきっているようだった。この男、演劇界に進んでいたらさぞかし素晴らしい俳優になっていただろう。実験室にいたら偉大な科学者になっていただろう。

We reached Miss Adler's home ten minutes before she was expected to return from the park. Lamps were being lit on the street and it was getting dark. But the street was not quiet. There was a group of men talking—they did not look respectable; a couple guards visiting with one of the girl servants and other well-dressed young men walking up and down the street.

"The photograph might be a problem for Miss Adler, too," Holmes said to me. "She probably does not want Mr. Norton to see it any more than the king wants his princess to see it. The question is, 'Where are we to find the photograph?'"

"She probably doesn't carry it with her. Too large. It is either with her banker or her lawyer. But remember, the king said that she wrote that she would use the photograph in a few days. It must be where she can lay her hands on it quickly. It must be in her own house."

"But the King sent robbers into her house twice, and they could not find it."

"Pshaw! They did not know where to look."

"But how will you look?"

"I will not look."

"What will you do?"

■ lit 動 light（点灯する）の過去分詞形　■ respectable 形 まともな、堅気の　■ well-dressed 形 身なりのよい　■ walk up and down 行ったり来たりする　■ any more それ以上　■ either A or B AかそれともB　■ lay one's hand on ～を入手［確保］する　■ robber 名 泥棒　■ pshaw 間 ふん！

　アドラー嬢が公園から戻る予定の時刻の10分前に、私たちは彼女の自宅に到着した。街灯に明りがともされ、夜の帳がおりつつあったが、通りは賑やかだった。男性の一団——上品とはいえない集団——がいた。二人の近衛兵が女中としゃべっていたり、めかしこんだ青年たちが通りを行ったりきたりしていた。

　「あの写真は、アドラー嬢にとってもやっかいなものだろう」とホームズが私に言った。「王が王女にあの写真を見られたくないのと同様、彼女だってきっとノートン氏に見られたくないだろうよ。問題は『写真はどこにあるか』だ。

　おそらく、持ち歩いているなんてことはないだろう。大きすぎる。銀行か、弁護士といったところか。でも王が言っていたことを考えると、彼女は写真を一両日中に使うつもりだと手紙に書いてきた。それなら、手元に置いているはずだ。自宅の中にね」

　「でも、王が二度も人を雇って自宅に押し入り、盗ませようとしたけれど、見つからなかったんだよ」
　「ふん、やつらは探すべき場所を知らないのだ」
　「でも、どうやって捜すんだ?」
　「捜しはしない」
　「ではどうするつもりだ?」

"I will get her to show it to me."

"She won't do that."

"She will. Here she comes. Do exactly as I told you."

Miss Adler's guards rushed up to her carriage to open the door for her. But some of the strange men on the street also came to the door, hoping to receive a small gift of money by helping the beautiful woman from her seat. They began to fight over who would help her. Holmes rushed into the crowd of men to protect Miss Adler, but just as he reached her, he gave a cry and fell to the ground, blood running down his face. Seeing blood, the rough men ran away and the kinder ones helped the lady to her house and attended to the injured man. Before going in her house, Miss Adler looked back into the street.

"Is the poor man hurt badly?" she asked.

"He is dead," someone said.

"No, he is still alive, but there is not much time," called out another.

"He's breathing now," said another. "What a kind man. Those rough men would have stolen your purse if he hadn't come running over to protect you. Can we bring him into your house for a moment, ma'am?"

"Of course."

■ get someone to（人）に〜してもらう ■ exactly 副 その通りに ■ rush up to 〜に
駆け上がる ■ strange man 見知らぬ男 ■ gift of money 寄付金 ■ fight over 〜を
めぐって言い争う ■ give a cry あっと叫ぶ ■ fall to the ground 転ぶ ■ rough 形
乱暴な ■ run away 走り去る、逃げる ■ kinder 形 kind（親切な）の比較級

「彼女に教えてもらうんだ」

「それは無理だろう」

「いや、教えてくれるさ。彼女が来たね。言ったとおりに行動してくれ」

アドラー嬢の近衛兵が馬車に駆け寄り、扉を開けた。しかし、通りにいた浮浪者たちも、美しい女性が馬車から降りるのを手伝って小銭を得ようと馬車に突進してきた。誰がその権利を得るかで喧嘩が始まった。変装したホームズはアドラー嬢を保護しようと、男たちの群れの中に飛び込んでいったが、彼女までたどりつく寸前に、叫び声を上げて倒れてしまった。顔からは血が流れていた。その血を見て、荒くれ男たちは逃げだし、親切な男たちが婦人を自宅へ連れていき、負傷した男を介抱した。家に入る前に、アドラー嬢は通りを振り返った。

「あの気の毒な男性のお怪我はひどいのでしょうか?」

「死んだよ」と誰かが言った。

「いや、まだ生きている。でも、時間の問題だ」と別の声があがった。

「まだ息はありますよ」とまた別の誰かが言った。「なんて親切な方でしょう。あの方があなたを守ろうと走ってこなかったら、あなたは乱暴な男たちにバッグを盗まれていましたよ。少しの間、お宅に運びこむわけにいきませんか、奥様?」

「もちろんです」

■ attend to（人）の手当てをする　■ injured 形 負傷した　■ breathe 動 呼吸する
■ stolen 動 steal（盗む）の過去分詞形　■ purse 名 小銭入れ　■ ma'am 名 ご婦人
《madamの縮約形》

I do not know how Holmes felt to be lying in her home with such a plan. I felt more ashamed than any other time in my life to be working against a lady of such grace and kindliness. I had promised him, though, so I hardened my heart and took out the smoke-rocket from under my overcoat. Holmes sat up and gave me the signal. I tossed my rocket into the room with a cry of "Fire!" Immediately, a whole crowd of people came to the house, but I ran to the street corner as I had agreed, and ten minutes later my friend joined me. We walked in silence for a few minutes.

"You did very well, Doctor," he finally said.

"Did you get the picture?"

"No, but I know where it is."

"How did you do it?"

"It was very simple. I splashed some red paint on my face. She felt sorry for me and had me brought into her house. But when a woman thinks that her house is on fire, she runs to the thing she values most. The smoke and shouting worked perfectly. She ran straight to the photograph behind a sliding panel in the wall. When I cried out that it was a false alarm and no real danger, she put the photograph back in the panel and rushed from the room. I also escaped from the house."

■ lying 動 lie（横たわる）の現在分詞形 ■ feel ashamed 恥ずかしいと思う ■ work against ～の足を引っ張る ■ grace 名 寛大さ、優しさ ■ kindliness 名 親切 ■ harden one's heart 心を鬼にする ■ take out 取り出す ■ smoke-rocket 名 発煙筒 ■ overcoat 名 外套 ■ sit up 起き上がる ■ give a signal 合図する

　ホームズがこんな方法を使って彼女の自宅に入り、横たわったままどう感じているのか、私にはわからない。しかし私は、このような慈悲深い親切な女性をわなにかけていることに、かつてないほどの羞恥心を感じていた。でも、私は彼と約束していたので、心を鬼にして、コートの下から発煙筒を取り出した。ホームズが起き上がり、こちらに合図を送った。私は発煙筒を投げ込み、「火事だ!」と叫んだ。またたくまに群衆が家に押し寄せ、私は約束した通りの角を目指して走った。そして10分後、友と落ち合った。私たちはしばらくの間、黙って歩いた。

　「すばらしかったよ、ワトソン先生」とホームズは口を開いた。
　「写真は手に入った?」
　「いや。でも場所はわかった」
　「どうやって?」
　「ごく簡単なことだよ。僕の顔の血は赤い絵の具さ。でも、彼女は気の毒に思って、家に入れてくれた。そして女性というものは、家が火事になったと思えば、自分が一番大切にしているもののところへ駆け寄る。煙と叫び声が完璧に作用したよ。彼女は壁の羽目板の後ろに隠した写真に駆け寄った。僕が誤報だ、危険はないと叫ぶと、彼女は写真を羽目板の後ろに戻し、部屋から走り出た。僕も部屋から抜け出したというわけさ」

■ toss 動 〜を軽く放る　■ immediately 副 すぐに　■ street corner 街角　■ in silence 無言で　■ splash 動（液体を）散らす　■ have someone do（人）に〜させる　■ on fire 火事になって　■ value 動 高く評価する　■ run straight to 〜に直行する　■ sliding panel スライド式パネル　■ false alarm 誤報、デマ

"Now what do we do?" I asked.

"We must visit with the King tomorrow. We will wait for her in the sitting room. But when she enters, she may find that both we and the photograph have gone. His Majesty would be pleased to regain the picture with his own hands."

"What time will we go?"

"At eight in the morning. Her marriage may change her life and habits completely."

3

We were having toast and coffee early the next morning when the King of Bohemia rushed into the room.

"Have you got it?"

"Not yet."

"But you have hopes?"

"I have hopes."

"Then let's go."

■ now 副 さて、ところで ■ regain 動 ～を取り戻す ■ habit 名 習慣 ■ toast 名 トースト ■ Not yet. 「いやまだ」

「それで、これからどうする?」

「明日、陛下と一緒に訪ねることにしよう。居間で彼女を待つことになると思う。彼女が入ってきた時には、僕らも写真も消えているというわけだ。陛下も写真を手元に取り戻せて、お喜びになることだろう」

「何時に行く?」

「朝8時。結婚して生活習慣がすっかり変わっているかもしれない」

3

翌朝早く、私たちがトーストとコーヒーを摂っていると、ボヘミア国王が部屋に駆け込んできた。

「手に入れたのか?」

「いいえ、まだです」

「だが、見込みはあるのだな」

「ええ、ございます」

「では、行こう」

"Irene Adler is married," Holmes said to the King.

"Married? To whom?"

"An English lawyer named Norton."

"But she could not love him."

"I hope she does."

"Why?"

"Because if she loves him, she does not love your Majesty. And if she does not love your Majesty, she will not interfere with your Majesty's plan."

"That is true. And yet—she would have made a wonderful queen. I wish she had been of my class…"

The king was silent until we reached Miss Adler's home, where an elderly woman was waiting at the door.

"Mr. Sherlock Homes, I believe?" said she.

"I am Mr. Holmes," answered my friend, looking at her in surprise.

"Indeed. Miss Adler told me you might come this morning. She left with her husband this morning for France."

"What? Do you mean that she is not in England?"

"And never coming back."

"We shall never get the photograph," cried the King.

"Let us look," said Holmes as he dashed into the house.

■ To whom?「誰と？」 ■ lawyer 图 弁護士 ■ interfere with ～を妨げる、～に干渉する ■ make 動 ～になる ■ S wish S' would have p.p. S' が～していたらなあ《仮定法過去完了》 ■ class 图 階級 ■ elderly 形 年配の ■ in surprise 驚いて ■ leave for ～に向かって出発する ■ dash into ～に駆け入る

40

「アイリーン・アドラーは結婚しました」とホームズは告げた。

「結婚だと？　誰とだ？」

「ノートンというイギリス人の弁護士です」

「彼女がそんな男を愛するはずがない」

「僕は、彼女がノートン氏を愛していることを望みます」

「なぜだ」

「なぜならば、彼女が彼を愛していれば、陛下を愛することはない。陛下を愛することがなければ、陛下の計画を邪魔することもないからです」

「その通りだ。だが、彼女なら素晴らしい妃になったことだろう。身分さえよければ……」

王はアドラー嬢の家に着くまで口を開かなかった。年配の女性が扉のところで待っていた。

「シャーロック・ホームズさんですね？」と彼女が言った。

「そうです。ホームズです」と友が答え、驚きに満ちたまなざしで彼女を見た。

「そうでしたか。奥様が、今朝あなたがお越しになるだろうとおっしゃったのです。奥様は旦那様と一緒に、今朝フランスへお発ちになりました」

「なんですと？　つまり彼女はイギリスにいないということですか？」

「ええ。二度とお戻りにはなりません」

「写真は取り戻せないのか」と王はうめいた。

「確かめましょう」とホームズは言って、家の中へ急いだ。

He tore open the panel and pulled out one photograph and one letter. It was a view of Miss Adler in an evening dress. The envelope of the letter was addressed to Mr. Sherlock Holmes. It read:

My dear Mr. Sherlock Holmes:

You are very clever. But after the fire I realized who you were. I had been warned about you several months ago. It was hard for me to be angry with a kind minister, as you seemed to be. But I also changed clothes and followed you to your door. Now that I know the King has asked you to help him, I talked to my husband and we decided it was best to leave England rather than deal with you.

Concerning the photograph, the King need not worry. I love and am loved by a better man than he. The king may do as he likes, and though he has been cruel to me, I will cause him no harm. I only keep the photograph so that he will not cause me trouble in future. The photograph he may keep if he likes. I remain, Mr. Holmes,

Yours most sincerely,
IRENE NORTON, *née* Adler.

■ tear open 引きはがして開ける　■ pull out 引き抜く　■ view 图 写真　■ evening dress イブニング・ドレス　■ be addressed to（郵便物など）を人にあてる　■ warn 動 警告する　■ be angry with（人）に腹を立てる　■ seem to be ～のように見える ■ rather than ～よりはむしろ　■ deal with（人と）折り合いを付ける

羽目板をひきはがすと、写真と手紙があった。引っ張り出してみると、イヴニング・ドレス姿のアイリーン・アドラーの姿だった。封筒の宛名は、シャーロック・ホームズ様となっていた。文面は次のとおりである。

親愛なるシャーロック・ホームズ様
　あなたは大変に頭の切れるお方でございます。でも、火事の後で、私はあなたの真の姿に気付いたのです。数ヵ月ほど前、警告されたことがありました。あの親切な牧師様——あなたは本当にうまく演じていらっしゃった——を悪く思うのは辛いことでした。でも、私自身も変装してあなたの後をつけ、お宅の戸口まで行き、そして、陛下があなたに助けを求めたことを知りました。私は夫に相談し、あなたと闘うよりもイギリスを去るのが良いだろうと決めたのでございます。
　写真については、陛下のご心配にはおよびません。私はもっと素晴らしい人を愛し、愛されています。陛下はお心のままになさいませ。陛下は私に冷酷な仕打ちをなさいましたけれども、私は陛下の邪魔をするようなことはいたしません。私は例の写真を持っていきますが、それは、陛下が私の未来の邪魔をなさらないようにするため、それだけのことです。こちらの写真は、陛下がお望みならばお持ち下さい。ではこれで失礼いたします。
　　　　　　　　親愛なるシャーロック・ホームズ様へ
　　　　　　　　アイリーン・ノートン（旧姓アドラー）

■ concerning 前 ～に関して　■ may 助 ～して差し支えない《許可》　■ cruel 形 残酷な、非情な　■ cause no harm 無害である　■ I remain yours sincerely. 敬具《手紙の結句》　■ née 形 旧姓～

Reading the letter, the King cried out, "Oh, what a woman! Wouldn't she have made an admirable queen?"

"She is indeed very clever," Holmes said. "I am sorry that I was not able to successfully get back your photograph."

"On the contrary," said the King, "she is a woman of honor and I now understand that the photograph is as safe as if I had thrown it into the fire."

"I am glad to hear your Majesty say so."

"And I would like to give you anything you ask. How about this emerald ring I am wearing?"

"Your Majesty has something I would value even more."

"Please name it."

"This photograph."

The King stared at Holmes in amazement.

"Irene's photograph? Certainly, if you wish."

"I thank your Majesty. There is no more to be done. I wish you a good-morning." Bowing, we returned to Holmes's rooms.

That was the only time I can remember that Holmes's plans were ruined by a woman. Since then, I have never heard him laugh about women. When he speaks of Irene Adler, it is always as *the* woman.

■ admirable 形 立派な ■ on the contrary それどころか ■ honor 名 高潔 ■ as if あたかも〜かのように ■ name 動 指定する ■ stare at 〜を凝視する ■ in amazement あっけに取られて ■ certainly 副 もちろん ■ bow 動 おじぎする ■ since then それ 以来 ■ laugh about 〜について笑う

　手紙を読み、王が叫んだ。「なんという女だ！　彼女なら素晴らしい王妃となったのではなかろうか」

　「本当に賢いお方です」とホームズが言った。「写真を取り戻すことができなかったことを遺憾に思います」

　「その逆だ」と王は言った。「彼女は高潔な女性だ。今、私は確信している。写真のことは心配する必要はない。火にくべたようなものだということをね」

　「陛下にそう言っていただき、大変嬉しく思います」
　「礼をしたい。このエメラルドの指輪はどうだ？」

　「陛下はもっと価値あるものをお持ちです」
　「それは何か？」
　「この写真です」
　王は驚いて、ホームズを見つめた。
　「アイリーンの写真だと？　よろしい。望むのであればもっていきなさい」
　「ありがたく存じます。この事件は解決しました。ごきげんよう」と陛下に一礼すると、私と一緒に自宅へ戻った。

　これが、ホームズの計画がひとりの女性によって破綻させられた、私が憶えている限り唯一の事件である。それ以来、ホームズが女性に関して軽んじたことを言うのを聞いたことがない。彼がアイリーン・アドラーについて話すときはいつも、「あの女性（ひと）」という敬称を使うのである。

覚えておきたい英語表現

> In his eyes she represents the very best of all women. （p.8, 2行目）
> 彼の目には、彼女はこの世で最高の女性に映っているのだ。

【解説】In his eyes は、「彼の目には」という意味です。「Beauty is in the eye of the beholder.（美は見る人の目の中にある）」という表現があるように、美しさとは、主観的なものであることを示しています。represents ～ は、「～を表わす、象徴する」という意味です。
the very best of all ～ は、「すべての～の中でも、最高の」という意味の、最上級の褒め言葉です。

【例文】① In her eyes, her husband was the kindest man in the world.
　　　　彼女の目には、夫が世界一やさしい男性に映った。

　　　② You are the very best of all employees I have ever had.
　　　　君は、私がこれまで雇った社員の中で最高だ。

> How I missed my friend. （p.10, 下から6行目）
> 友に会いたくなった。

【解説】miss ～ は、「～がいないのを寂しく思う、なつかしく思う」の意味です。この文章を直訳すると、「友人のことがむしょうになつかしく思えた」となります。

【例文】① I will miss you.
　　　　君がいなくなると寂しいよ。　　＊お別れのときに言うせりふです。

　　　② I really missed you!
　　　　寂しかったわ！　　　　　　　＊再会のときに言うせりふです。

> I think you have gained seven and a half pounds since I last saw you. （p.12, 4行目）
> 最後に会ったときから7.5ポンド増えたようだな。

【解説】日本語では、「太った」という言葉を使いますが、英語では、体重をgain（獲

得) したという表現を使います。または、put on weight(体重を増やす) という言い
方もあります。fat(太る) という言葉を使うのはタブーですから、気をつけましょう。

【例文】① I gained 10 pounds in two weeks! So, I need to lose 15 pounds by
Christmas.
2週間で10ポンドも増えちゃった! クリスマスまでに15ポンド減量しなきゃ。

② I must go on diet because I gained 2 pounds.
2ポンド増えたからダイエットしなくては。

Only do as I instruct you. （p.28, 下から2行目）
僕が指示したことだけをしてほしいんだ。

【解説】instructは、「指示する、教える」の意味です。
Do as I ～ you. は、「私が君に～したようにしてくれ」の命令形です。

【例文】① Please do as I say.
私が言った通りにしてください。

② Instruct me how I can solve this puzzle.
この謎を解く方法を教えてください。

They did not look respectable. （p.32, 4行目）
上品とはいえない集団。

【解説】ネガティブなコメントをする際に、not ～と、notのあとにポジティブな単語
を入れると、上品な文章になります。
respectableは、「品のいい、尊敬すべき」という意味です。

【例文】① Behave in a respectable way.
きちんとした行動をせよ。

② I am afraid your comment is not quite respectable.
残念ながら、君のコメントは尊重しかねるね。
＊失礼なことを言った相手に対して、こんな言い方で返すのはいかが?

THE RED-HEADED LEAGUE

今日の依頼人は燃えるような赤毛の質屋の主人だ。
「赤毛組合」という不思議な組合の会員に選ばれ、1日4時間、
百科事典を筆写するだけで週給4ポンド（約10万円）という
夢のような仕事にありついたのだが、
その組合が突然無くなってしまったので調べてほしいという……

『ボヘミアの醜聞』の翌月、『ストランド』誌に掲載された2番目の作品。
前回の依頼人は国王だったが、今回は質屋の主人。
依頼内容も写真を取り戻すことから、不可解な身の回りの出来事の解明に
なっているが、あふれるサスペンスと、あっと驚く結末は変わらない。
この作品によりホームズの人気は不動のものになった。

ホームズ物語のなかでも1、2を争う傑作で、これ以後、
この奇抜なトリックを使った多くの小説や映画が生まれている。

赤毛組合

The Red-headed League

It was one day last fall. I called on my friend, Mr. Sherlock Holmes. He was deep in conversation with a stout, older man who had red hair. I thought I should leave and turned away, but Holmes took my arm and pulled me into the room, closing the door.

"You have come at a perfect time, my dear Watson," he said with a smile.

"You seem to be busy."

"And so I am."

"Then I can wait in the next room."

"Not at all. Mr. Wilson, please allow me to introduce my friend, Mr. Watson, who helps me in all my work. I think he will help me on your case, too."

■ call on（人）を訪問する　■ be deep in conversation 話し込んでいる　■ stout 形 かっぷくがいい　■ turn away 背を向ける　■ Not at all. 「とんでもない」

50

赤毛組合

　去年の秋のある日のこと。友人のシャーロック・ホームズ宅を訪れたら、彼はがっちりした年上の赤髪の男と話し込んでいる最中だった。失礼したほうが良いと思い帰りかけたが、ホームズがドアを閉めつつ、私の腕を取って部屋に引き戻した。

　「丁度いいところに来てくれたよ、ワトソン君」ホームズが笑いながら言った。

　「忙しそうだな」

　「その通りだ」

　「では隣室で待とう」

　「それには及ばないよ。ウィルソンさん、友人のワトソンを紹介させてください。私の扱う事件全部で手伝ってもらっています。あなたの事件でも助けてくれると思いますよ」

The stout man stood up and bowed to me quickly with small eyes which seemed to have a questioning look.

"Please sit on the sofa," Holmes said to me as he sat in his usual chair. "I know that you are interested in my unusual cases, so different from the humdrum routine of everyday life, because you have written so many of them into stories."

"Your cases have always been of interest to me, it is true," I replied.

"You will recall just the other day, I told you that life itself has the most unusual situations, more daring than we can even imagine."

"And I doubted you."

"You did, Doctor, but I will give you so many facts that you will come around to seeing things my way soon. Now, Mr. Wilson here has come to visit me this morning and tell me a story. I have often told you, Watson, that the strangest things often happen with the smallest crimes. I have not heard his whole story yet, but it seems that it is the most unusual story I have ever been told.

■ stand up 立ち上がる ■ a questioning look いぶかしげな顔つき ■ sofa 图 長椅子
■ humdrum 形 単調な、退屈な ■ be of interest to ～にとって興味深い ■ recall 動
思い出す ■ the other day 先日、この間 ■ daring 形 大胆な ■ doubt 動 ～を疑う
■ come around 意見を変える

　がっちりした男は立ち上がって、すばやく一礼したが、その小さな目は不審げであった。

　「ソファにかけてくれ」ホームズはいつもの自分の椅子に座りながら、私に言った。「君は、僕が扱う、平凡な日常とはかけ離れた、変わった事件に興味を持っているね。沢山の事件を話として記録したからね」

　「君の扱う事件には、つねに興味があるよ。それは本当だ」私は答えた。

　「つい先日も君に言ったじゃないか、人生そのものの方が、最も奇異で、我々の想像を超える大胆な状況をはらんでいるものだと」

　「そして私はそれを疑問視した」
　「そうだ、ドクター、しかし沢山の事実を君に示して、君もすぐに考えを変えて私と同じ見方をするようにしよう。ここにいるウィルソン氏は今朝、ある話をしに来てくれた。君に何度も言ったように、最も奇妙な出来事というのは、最も軽微な犯罪に伴って起きるものだよ。ウィルソン氏の話はまだ全部を聞いたわけではないが、今まで耳にした中で一番風変わりなもののようだ」

"Mr. Wilson, please begin your story again. I ask you to do this not only for Mr. Watson, but also because it is such an unusual story, I would like to hear every word again from your lips. Usually, when I begin to study a case, I think of thousands of other cases like it, and I am guided in my decisions. But in this case, I cannot think of a single one which is similar. The facts are, as best I can tell, unique."

Then the heavy man pulled a piece of newspaper from his inside pocket. He spread the advertisement section on his knee. I looked at him carefully, trying to understand what kind of a man he was.

But I could understand very little. He seemed a very average laborer, overweight, proud, and slow. His clothes were old and unclean. The only unusual thing about him was his blazing red hair and the unhappy look on his face.

Sherlock Holmes was watching me. He smiled, "I can tell that Mr. Wilson has been a laborer, that he believes in God, that he has been to China and that recently he has done a lot of writing. Otherwise I can tell nothing about him."

Mr. Wilson was surprised to hear Holmes say all this.

"How do you know all that about me?"

■ think of ～を思い付く　■ similar 形 似ている　■ advertisement 名 広告　■ knee 名 ひざ　■ very little ほんの少し　■ average 形 普通の　■ laborer 名 労働者　■ overweight 形 太り過ぎの　■ unclean 形 汚れた　■ blazing 形 赤々と燃え上がる　■ recently 副 最近　■ writing 名 書くこと、執筆　■ otherwise 副 その他の点では

「ウィルソンさん、もう一度最初から話してください。ワトソン氏のためだけではなく、あまりに風変わりな話ですから、私自身もあなたの口から再度、一言一句を聞きたいのです。通常は事件の調査を始めたら、何千もの似たようなケースを思い浮かべて参考にすることができる。しかし今回は、類似したケースなど一つも思いつかない。関係する諸事実は、どう表現しても、特異であるとしか言いようがない」

そこで大柄な男は背広の内ポケットから新聞のページを引っ張り出し、膝の上に広告欄を置いた。私は、どういう人間かを見定めようとして、彼を注意深く観察した。

だが読み取れたのはごくわずかだった。どこにでもいる労働者階級の男で、肥満、プライドは高く、頭の回転は鈍そうだった。着ている服は、古くて薄汚れている。唯一、変わっているのは、燃えるような赤毛と、惨めな顔つきだった。

シャーロック・ホームズは私を観察していた。彼は笑って、「ウィルソンさんが労働者で、信心深く、中国に行ったことがあり、最近大量の書き物をしたということはわかっている。ほかには何もわからない」と言った。

ウィルソン氏は、ホームズがこれだけ述べるのを聞いて驚いた様子だった。「どうしてそんなに私のことがわかるんですか?」

"Well," Holmes began, "the muscles of your right hand are much more developed. So you have worked hard with it. The coat pin shows your religious interest. The lower five inches of your right sleeve is shiny because you have moved it along your writing paper as you sat at a desk writing, while the left elbow is thin where you rested it on the desk."

"What about China?"

"I see an inked mark on your hand which could only have been painted in China. That light pink color only comes out of China. I also see a Chinese coin on your watch chain. It was all very simple."

Mr. Wilson laughed loudly. "Well, at first I thought there was some magic, but I see it is very simple."

"I wonder if I should tell all my secrets, Watson. No one will be impressed with me any more if I tell everything. Can't you find the advertisement, Mr. Wilson?"

"Yes, I have got it here," he said marking it with his finger. "Please read it for yourself."

Holmes took the paper and began to read:

■ muscle 图 筋肉 ■ developed 形 発達した ■ coat pin（胸の）飾りピン ■ religious 形 宗教的な ■ elbow 图 ひじ ■ inked mark 入れ墨 ■ come out of ～から採れる ■ I wonder if I should ～した方がいいかなあ ■ be impressed with ～に感銘を受ける ■ mark 動（指し）示す ■ for oneself 自力で

「うむ」ホームズは始めた。「あなたの右手の筋肉は左より余程発達しています。右腕で重労働をしたのでしょう。コートについている記章は宗教心の現れです。右袖の端5インチがテカテカに光っているのは、机に向かって書き物をした時に紙の上をこすったからで、左の肘は逆に机に乗せていたために擦り切れている」

「中国についてはどうなんです?」
「手に刺青がありますが、これは中国でしか入れられないものです。そのうすいピンク色は、中国でしか採れない。時計の鎖にも中国の硬貨がぶら下がっている。というわけで、ごく単純なことなのですよ」

ウィルソン氏は大笑いした。「ははあ、最初はなんか魔法でも使ったのかと思いましたが、単純なんですな」
「手の内をばらしてしまうのは考えものだな、ワトソン君。全部喋ったら、感銘を受ける人間がいなくなるじゃないか。広告がみつからないのですか、ウィルソンさん?」
「ありましたとも」指で差しながら言った。「ご自分で読んでください」

ホームズは紙切れを手に取って読み上げた。

"Opening for one red-headed man. Must be healthy and strong, over twenty-one years old. Easy work. Pay: four pounds a week. Apply in person on Monday, at eleven o'clock, to Duncan Ross, at the office of the League, 7 Pope's Court, Fleet Street."

"What does it mean?" I asked.

Holmes laughed with pleasure. "It is unusual, isn't it? And now, Mr. Wilson, tell us the effect that this advertisement had on your life. Note the date of the paper, Watson."

"It is *The Morning Chronicle* of April 27, 1890. Just two months ago."

"Very good. Now, Mr. Wilson?"

"Well, I have a small pawnshop in London, but I do not earn much money there. I used to have two helpers, but now I can have only one. Even he comes for only half pay to learn the business."

"His name?"

"Vincent Spaulding. I know he could earn more somewhere else, but if he wants to work for me, I will not say anything."

"Yes, you are lucky to get someone to work for you at less than the normal pay. I think he may be as unusual as the advertisement you have read us."

■ opening for（人）の空き［欠員］ ■ apply 動 申し込む ■ in person 本人が直接に ■ league 名 連盟、協会 ■ note 動 〜に注意［注目］する ■ pawnshop 名 質屋 ■ used to 以前は〜していた ■ earn 動 金を得る

「求む、赤毛の男性一名。健康で強健、21歳以上であること。単純
労働。給与:週4ポンド。月曜日11時に来所の上、応募のこと。フリー
ト街、ポープス・コート7番地、組合事務所のダンカン・ロスまで」

「これはどういうことです?」私は尋ねた。

ホームズは嬉しそうに笑った。「本当に変わってるだろう? ではウィルソン
さん、次に広告があなたの人生をどう変えたか、話してください。新聞の日付
に気をつけてくれ、ワトソン君」

「モーニング・クロニクル紙、1890年4月27日付だ。丁度2ヵ月前だな」

「よろしい。ではウィルソンさん?」

「私はロンドンで小さな質屋をやっとりますが、ほとんど儲かりません。以
前は2人雇っていましたが、今は1人しか置けません。その男も、商売を覚え
るためということで半値で来るから雇えるんでして」

「雇い人の名は何といいますか?」

「ヴィンセント・スポールディングです。よそへ行けばもっと稼げるはずな
んですが、うちで働きたいっていうんだから、こちらは何も言わないでおくこ
とにしたのです」

「通常より安い給料で働いてもいいという人間がいたのはラッキーでした
ね。今の広告と同じぐらい奇特な奴だとは思いますがね」

"Oh, he is all right, but he has his problems. He is always taking pictures. Then he runs downstairs to develop them. But generally he works hard."

"He is working for you now?"

"Yes, he and a girl of fourteen live with me. She cooks and keeps the place clean. I have no other family alive. We live very quiet lives. It was that advertisement that changed everything. Spaulding brought it to me saying, 'I wish I had red hair, Mr. Wilson.'

" 'Why?' I asked.

" 'This job at the League of the Red-headed Men—it is such easy work and so well-paid. They always need more men than they can find.'

"You see, Mr. Holmes, I am a stay-at-home man. My business came to me, and I often spend weeks in my home and office without even going outside. But Spaulding kept telling me about this job. So I asked him, 'What kind of a job is it?'

" 'It is very easy and you can continue working as you are now. But you will be paid a couple hundred pounds a year extra.'

"Then I began to be interested, because the money would be useful.

" 'Tell me about it,' I said.

■ develop 動（フィルムを）現像する ■ generally 副 大抵、通常 ■ keep ~ clean ~をきれいな状態に保つ ■ well-paid 形 賃金の高い ■ stay-at-home 形 家の中にばかりいる、出無精の ■ my business come to me 仕事の方からやってくる ■ extra 副 余分に

「奴は大丈夫ですよ。問題点もありますがね。四六時中、写真を撮っては地下に走って行って現像してやがる。だが全体としてはよくできた店員ですよ」

「今もあなたのところで働いているのですか?」
「そうです。奴と14歳の小娘が住み込みで、娘が料理と掃除をするんで。私には他に生き残った家族もいないので、3人で静かに暮らしています。あの広告が何もかも変えちまったんです。スポールディングがあれを持ってきて、『俺の髪も赤かったらなあ、ウィルソンさん』と言うので。

『なぜだ?』と聞いたら、
『この赤毛の男のための赤毛組合の仕事は楽な上に給料がいいんですよ。なのにいつも雇える人材が足りないんです』

よろしいですか、ホームズさん。私は家でじっとしてるのが好きなんです。仕事が向こうからやってきたんですよ。何週間も外へ出ずに、家と仕事場だけで過ごすこともあります。だがスポールディングがしつこく言うもんで、聞いたんですよ、『どんな仕事なんだ?』って。
『ものすごく簡単で、今の仕事も続けられるんですよ。それで、年に200ポンド余分に稼げるんですからね』
それで私も気になりだした、その金は使い勝手がありそうですから。

『詳しく話してくれ』と言いました。

" 'The League was founded by an American millionaire who felt sympathy for other red-headed men. He left all his money to a club which has the power to give money to any red-headed man.'

" 'But there must be thousands of men asking for the money.'

" 'No, not so many, because your hair must be blazing, not light red, or dark red. I am sure that you would get some of their money if you went to the Fleet Street office next Monday, Sir.'

"I decided to try for the position. I asked Spaulding to lock up the house and shop and come with me. He was happy to have a day off work.

"Well, on the following Monday at eleven o'clock, every man who had even a little red in his hair had marched into London from north, south, east and west and come to the office of the League. There was every color of red: strawberry, lemon, orange, brick, Irish-setter, liver, clay. But no one had that flaming color that Spaulding talked about and was mentioned in the advertisement. When I saw all those men, I wanted to go home immediately, but Spaulding wouldn't let me. He pulled me through the crowd and into the office. We had to push through hundreds of bodies."

"Such an interesting story," Holmes commented. "Please continue."

■ found 動 ～を設立する ■ sympathy 名 同情 ■ ask for ～を求める ■ try for ～を獲得しようとする ■ position 名 身分、職業 ■ lock up （ドアなどに）鍵を掛ける ■ day off work （平日に取る）休日 ■ march into ～に進撃する ■ brick 名 れんが

『この組合ってやつは、ほかの赤毛の男に同情したアメリカの百万長者が設立したもので、遺産を全部この組合に残して、赤毛の男には誰でも資金援助できるようにしたんですよ』

『だが、金を欲しがる赤毛の男なんぞ、何千人もいるんじゃないか』

『いや、そんなに多くありませんよ。燃え立つような赤でなくちゃならないんで、薄い赤や暗い赤では駄目なんです。来週月曜日にフリート街の事務所に行かれたら、きっと金が入りますよ』

そこで私は応募することにしたんです。スポールディングにも、家と店を閉めて一緒に来るように頼みました。やつは一日仕事を休んで嬉しそうでしたよ。

そして次の月曜日の11時が来ると、まあほんのちょっと赤が混じっているだけのような髪の奴でも、北から、南から、東から、西から、組合事務所めがけて来るは、来るは。ありとあらゆる赤毛がいましたよ。イチゴ色、レモン色、オレンジ色、レンガ色、アイリッシュ・セッター犬の色、肝臓色、粘土色。だが、スポールディングが言っていて、広告にあったような燃え立つ赤は見当たりません。あまりの人の多さに、私はすぐに家に帰りたかったのですが、スポールディングが聞かないんですよ。群衆をぬって事務所まで私を引っ張っていき、何百もの人間のあいだを通り抜ける破目になりました」

「なんとも興味深い話だ」ホームズは述べた。「続けてください」

■ Irish-setter 名 アイリッシュ・セッター《赤い毛を持つ犬の品種》 ■ liver 名 レバー、茶褐色 ■ clay 名 粘土 ■ flaming 形 燃え立つ（ように赤い） ■ mention 動 ～に言及する ■ comment 動 コメントする

"There was one man behind a desk. Every red-headed man who came up to him, he asked a question and then sent him away. It seemed to be very difficult to get this job. However, when Spaulding and I entered, he closed the door behind us so we could talk privately.

"'This is Mr. Jabez Wilson,' said my assistant. 'He is willing to fill your position.'

"'And he is well-qualified for the job,' the man behind the desk added. He stood staring for a long time at my hair until I felt embarrassed. Then suddenly he jumped forward and shook my hand, congratulating me on my success.

"'Now, please excuse me. I must check on your hair,' he said. Then he began to pull on my hair very hard. I yelled with pain and he stopped, saying, 'I see that it is real hair. There are tears in your eyes.'

"Then he went to the open window and shouted down to the crowd that the vacancy was filled. There was a groan of disappointment from below as everyone began to move away from the building.

"'My name is Duncan Ross. I am glad to meet you. Do you have a family, Mr. Wilson?'

"I answered that I did not.

■ come up to ～にやって来る　■ send someone away （人）をどこかに追い払う　■ be willing to ～する意思［用意］がある　■ well-qualified 形 資質の高い　■ feel embarrassed 決まりの悪い思いをする　■ forward 副 前へ、前方に　■ shook 動 shake（～を振る）の過去形　■ congratulate 動 （人に）祝いの言葉を述べる

「事務所には男が一人、机の向こうに座って、どの赤毛の男も、一言質問しては追い払っていました。この勤め口はちょっとやそっとでは得られないようでした。だが、スポールディングと私が入ると、男は内密に話ができるようにドアまで閉めたんです。

『こちら、ジャベズ・ウィルソンさんです』私の助手が言った。『勤め口を希望してます』

『それに条件をよく満たしている』机のむこうの男が付け加えました。男は立って私の髪を長いこと眺めるので、赤面するほどでした。そして急に前にでて、私の手を握り、就職おめでとうと言うんですよ。

『今一度、失礼して、あなたの髪をチェックさせて頂きますよ』彼は言って、私の髪を強く引っ張り始めました。痛くて叫んだら、『本物の毛髪に間違いありません。涙が出ていますね』と言いながらやっと止めました。

その後、男は開いた窓から通りに向かって、空きは無くなったと群衆に告げました。失望のうなり声とともに、群衆は消えていきました。

『私はダンカン・ロス。お会い出来て光栄です。ウィルソンさん、ご家族は?』

私はいないと答えました。

■ excuse 動 許す、容赦する　■ pull on ～を引っ張る　■ yell 動 大声で叫ぶ　■ shout down 大声をたてて（人を）黙らせる　■ vacancy 名 欠員　■ groan 名 うめき声　■ disappointment 名 失望、落胆　■ move away from ～から離れる

"'Dear me!' he said quietly, 'that is very serious indeed! I am sorry to hear you say that. This money was given to our organization so that more red-headed sons might be born.'

"I was afraid that I did not have the job, then he said: 'However, your hair is so unusually red, that we will allow you to join us anyway. When can you begin your new duties?'

"'It is a little difficult,' I said, 'for I have a business already. What are these hours?'

"'Ten to two.'

"'I will take care of your pawnshop,' Spaulding broke in.

"Now, a pawnshop is busy mostly on Thursday and Friday evenings, just before payday, Mr. Holmes, so I thought that I would be able to work midday at the office with Mr. Ross. And I knew that my assistant was a good man and could take care of our office.

"'That would suit me,' I replied. 'And the work?'

"'Is purely nominal.'

"'What do you call purely nominal?'

"'Well, you have to be in the office, or at least in the building, the whole time. If you leave, you lose your position forever.'

"'Only four hours a day, though. That is not a problem.'

"'No excuse will be allowed.'

"'And the work?'

■ Dear me! 「おや！」《驚きや感動を示す》 ■ organization 名 組織、団体 ■ however 副 しかしながら ■ anyway 副 とにかく ■ for 接 ～だから ■ take care of ～を引き受ける ■ break in 口を挟む ■ payday 名 給料日 ■ midday 名 真昼、白昼 ■ suit 動 適合する ■ purely 副 純粋に ■ nominal 形 名目上の ■ excuse 名 言い訳

『なんてことだ!』ダンカン・ロスは静かに言った。『これは実にゆゆしい事態だ! ご家族がいないとは残念です。組織の資金は、もっと赤毛の息子たちが増えるようにという目的で与えられているのですからね』

私は、これで仕事はおじゃんかと恐れましたが、男は『しかしながらあなたの髪は本当に稀な赤さですから、とりあえず加入を許可しましょう。仕事はいつから始められますか?』

『ちょっと問題があります』私は言った。『実はもう仕事についているんで。こちらはどういう時間帯なんですか?』

『10時から2時です』

『私が店番しますよ』スポールディングが割って入りました。

質屋というのは、給料日前の木曜日と金曜日の夜が忙しいんですよ。ホームズさん、だから私は日中はロスさんのところで働けると思いました。アシスタントはいい奴で、店番もちゃんとできるってわかっていましたし。

『その時間なら来られます』私は答えた。『で、仕事内容は?』

『形ばかりのものですよ』

『形ばかりとは?』

『まず、勤務時間中は事務所に、少なくともこの建物内にいなくてはならない。建物から出れば、この職を永久に失います』

『一日4時間だけでしょう。問題ありませんよ』

『言い訳はなしですよ』

『それで、仕事内容は?』

" 'To copy the Encyclopedia Britannica. You must bring your own paper and pen. But we will give you a desk and chair. Can you start tomorrow?'

" 'Certainly.'

" 'Then, goodbye, Mr. Wilson, and congratulations. You have won a very important position for yourself.'

"I was very pleased with my new job. But I thought about it later after coming home and I began to feel bad about it. I thought it must be some trick. Who would pay someone so much money for doing such easy work? In the morning, however, I bought a bottle of ink and some paper and went over to Mr. Ross's office.

"The table was ready for me. Mr. Duncan came into my room from time to time. At two o'clock, he said good-bye and was pleased that I had copied so many pages.

"This continued for a long time. Every Saturday, the manager gave me four gold coins and every morning I came in at ten and every afternoon I left at two.

"Eight weeks passed like this and then suddenly the whole business came to an end."

"To an end?"

"Yes, sir. It was just this morning. I went to my work as usual, but the door was shut and locked, with this note on it":

■ Encyclopedia Britannica ブリタニカ百科事典　■ congratulations 圃 おめでとう ■ feel bad about ～を不愉快に思う　■ trick 图 ごまかし、たくらみ　■ go over to ～に 出向いて行く　■ come to an end 終わる

『ブリタニカ百科事典を手書きで写すこと。紙とペンは持参してください。机と椅子はこちらで用意します。明日から始められますね?』

『もちろん』

『ではさようなら、ウィルソンさん。おめでとう。大変重要な仕事の口を獲得されたのですよ』

　私は新しい仕事が嬉しかったんです。だが家に帰って後で考えたら、嫌な感じがしてきました。なにかのトリックがあるはずだと思いました。でなければ、誰があんな単純労働にあんな大金を出す?　だが朝になるとやっぱり、インク瓶と紙を買って、ロスさんの事務所へ行きました。

　机は準備できていました。ダンカンさんは時々私の部屋に顔を出します。午後2時になるとさよならを言い、私が沢山のページを複写したのを見て喜びました。

　これが長いこと続きました。土曜ごとにマネージャーが金貨を4枚くれて、私は毎朝10時に来て午後2時に帰りました。

　8週間がこんな調子で過ぎたあと、突然、何もかもが終わってしまったのです」

　「終わり?」

　「そうです、旦那。今朝のことですよ。いつもの通り仕事に行ったら、ドアには鍵がかかってて、こんな張り紙がしてあったのです」

THE RED-HEADED LEAGUE
IS
DISSOLVED.
October 9, 1890

Sherlock Holmes and I both read the note over and then broke out laughing.

"I do not think it is funny," our man said. "I can go somewhere else if you are just going to laugh."

"No, please don't go," said Holmes. "It is just so unusual. Tell us, what did you do when you found this note?"

"I went down to the ground floor and asked the landlord what had happened to the Red-headed League. He said that he had never heard of any such body. Then I asked him who Mr. Duncan Ross was.

"'Oh, he was a lawyer. He was using the room upstairs until his new office was ready. At 17 King Edward Street, near St. Paul's.'

"I went to that address, Mr. Holmes, but it was a different company and I could not find Mr. Ross."

"What did you do then?"

"I asked my assistant to help me, but he did not know what else to do, so I have come to you for help."

■ dissolve 動 解散する ■ read over 通読する ■ break out laughing ドッと笑いだす ■ funny 形 おかしい ■ ground floor 1階 ■ landlord 名 家主 ■ body 名 組織、団体 ■ upstairs 名 上階

赤毛組合は
1890年10月9日を持って
解散しました。

シャーロック・ホームズと私は張り紙を読んで、それから吹き出した。

「面白くなんかありませんよ」男は言った。「笑いものにするんなら、他へ行ってもいいんですから」

「いやいや、頼むから行かないでください」ホームズは言った。「あんまり変わっているものですからね。聞かせてください、これを見てどうしました?」

「一階に降りて、家主に赤毛組合はどうなったのかと聞きました。家主はそんな団体は聞いたことがないと言う。それでダンカン・ロスってのは誰かと聞いたんです。

『弁護士だったがね、新しい事務所が準備できるまで、上の部屋を使ってたんだよ。事務所はセント・ポール寺院のそばのキングエドワード街17番地だよ』

私はその住所へ行ってみましたよ、ホームズさん。でも全然違う会社が入っていて、ロスって人はみつかりませんでした」

「それでどうしました?」

「助手に助けを頼みましたが、奴もどうしていいかわかりません。だからあなたのところに助けてもらいに来たんです」

"I am happy to look into your case. I think it may be more serious than you expect."

"More serious? Why, I have lost four pound a week."

"I do not think you can complain against the League. You have earned thirty pounds and learned some of the Encyclopedia. But we will try to clear up things. How long had you known your assistant before he found this ad?"

"About a month."

"How did he come?"

"In answer to an advertisement."

"Why did you pick him?"

"Because he came at half-wages."

"Are his ears pierced for earrings?"

"Yes."

"Is he still with you?"

"Oh, yes, I have just come from the pawnshop."

"Are you satisfied with his work in your absence?"

"Yes, there is not much to do during the day."

"That will be all for now, Mr. Wilson. Today is Saturday. On Monday I will give you my opinion on the subject."

"Well, Watson," said Holmes when our visitor had left us, "what do you think?"

"I cannot understand it at all," I told him.

■look into ～を調査する ■lost 動 lose（～を失う）の過去形 ■complain 動 苦情を申し立てる ■clear up 明らかにする ■ad 名 広告 ■pick 動 選ぶ ■pierced 形 穴のあいた ■be satisfied with ～に満足している ■absence 名 不在 ■all for now 今のところは（これで）結構です

「あなたのケースを喜んで扱いましょう。あなたが考えているより深刻だと思いますね」

「より深刻ですって？　私は週に4ポンドの収入を失くしたんですよ」

「組合に苦情を言えるとは思えませんね。あなたは30ポンド稼いで、百科事典の内容も勉強になった。だが物事をはっきりさせるとしましょう。あの広告を見つけるまで、助手のことはどのくらいの期間、知っていましたか？」

「一ヵ月ほど」

「どういう経緯で雇うことになったのですか？」

「こちらが出した広告に応募してきたのです」

「なぜ彼を選んだのですか？」

「半値でいいと言うからですよ」

「彼の耳にはピアスの穴がありますか？」

「はい」

「まだあなたのところで働いているのですか？」

「ええ、今も私は店から来たんで」

「あなたの留守中の仕事ぶりは満足のいくものですか？」

「はい、日中はひまですし」

「今日はこれまで、ウィルソンさん。今日は土曜日。月曜日になったらこの件についての見解をお伝えしましょう」

「なあ、ワトソン君」客が帰ると、ホームズが言った。「君はどう思う？」

「私には全くわからん」と答えた。

"Yes, all very strange. I must think quickly," he said, curling up in a chair and closing his eyes.

I thought he was falling asleep and I was, too. Then he jumped up, "There is a German concert this afternoon. Can you leave your patients, Doctor?"

"Oh, yes, I am never busy on Saturday."

"Then, let us take lunch on the way. Come along."

We took the subway to Aldersgate and then a short walk to the small building that Mr. Wilson had told us about that morning. We saw a brown board with JABEZ WILSON in white letters. Holmes walked up and down the street, studying the buildings. Then he walked up the street to the pawnshop and knocked at the door. A young man opened the door and asked us to come in.

"Thank you. I would just like to ask the way to the Strand from here."

"Third right, fourth left," said the assistant, closing the door.

"Smart man," Holmes said. "Fourth-smartest man in London."

"I am sure that he is important in our mystery. You wanted to see him, didn't you?" I asked.

"Not him, the knees of his trousers."

"What did you see?"

"My dear doctor, this is the time for observation, not for talk. We are spies in an enemy's country."

■ curl up 丸まる　■ fall asleep 眠り込む　■ German 形 ドイツ (音楽) の　■ leave 動 ～を放っておく　■ take lunch 食事を取る　■ on the way 途中で　■ come along 一緒に行く　■ subway 名 地下鉄　■ knock at the door ドアをノックする　■ observation 名 観察、観測　■ spy 名 スパイ

「そうだな、何もかも奇妙だ。早く考えをまとめなければ」ホームズは椅子に丸まって目を閉じながら言った。

彼は眠りかけているのだと思い、自分もうとうとしたところで、彼が飛び起きた。「ドイツ音楽のコンサートが今日の午後にあるんだ。患者はほうっておけるかい、ワトソン君?」

「大丈夫、土曜に忙しかった試しがない」

「では途中で昼食を取るとしよう。来たまえ」

我々は地下鉄でオルダーズゲイト（今のバービカン駅）まで行き、少し歩いて、今朝ウィルソン氏が話していた小さな建物に来た。茶色の板に「ジャベズ・ウィルソン」と白地で書いてあった。ホームズは、建物を観察しながら通りを行ったり来たりした。そして質屋の前まで来てドアをノックした。若い男がドアを開け、我々を中へ招いた。

「いや、ありがとう。ストランドに出る道を訪ねたいだけなのだが」

「三本目を右、四本目を左」ドアを閉めながら、助手は答えた。

「頭のいいやつだな」ホームズは言った。「ロンドンで四番目に頭がいい」

「今回のミステリーで大事な役割を果たしていることは間違いないな。どんな奴か、見てみたかったんだろう?」私は聞いた。

「奴じゃない、奴のズボンの膝だ」

「何が分かった?」

「君々、今は観察の時間であって、おしゃべりの時間じゃない。我々は敵地に潜入したスパイなんだぞ」

We turned the corner from the pawnshop, and we were on one of the most expensive streets in London. It was hard to believe they were so close.

"Just a minute," said Holmes. "I am trying to learn all the buildings in this neighborhood."

After a few moments, he said, "And now, Doctor, we have done our work. Let us have a sandwich and some coffee, and then off to musicland where all is sweetness and harmony."

Holmes completely enjoyed music. He would listen at home, waving his long arms in the air. This poetic mood was so different from the mood of Holmes when he worked on difficult cases and mysteries. Later that day, as we sat listening to the music at St. James's I thought that the people he was hunting were soon going to be very sorry.

After the concert, Holmes suggested that I go home. "But I will need your help tonight."

"At what time?"

"Ten will be early enough."

"I will see you at Baker Street at ten."

"Very well, but Doctor, there may be some danger, so put your gun in your pocket."

■ expensive 形 高級な ■ Just a minute.「ちょっと待って」 ■ off to 〜へ出掛ける ■ musicland 名 音楽の国 ■ sweetness 名 甘美 ■ harmony 名 調和、ハーモニー ■ poetic mood 詩的な雰囲気 ■ suggest 動 〜を提案する

質屋の角を曲がると、ロンドンでも最高級の通りに出た。こんな目と鼻の先にあるとは信じがたい。

「ちょっと待て」ホームズが言った。「この近隣のビルを全て覚えたいんだよ」

少しするとホームズは、「さあ、ドクター、仕事は終わりだ。サンドイッチとコーヒーを飲んで音楽の世界に浸ろう。すべてが甘く調和している音楽の世界に」

ホームズは音楽が心底好きだった。家では、長い両腕を振りながら聞いていた。この詩的な雰囲気は、難解な事件やミステリーに取り掛かっている時のホームズとは全く異なっていた。その日の午後、二人でセント・ジェームズ・ホールで音楽に耳を傾けていると、ホームズが追いつめようとしている連中は、まもなく非常に情けないことになるだろうという気がしてきた。

コンサートが終わると、ホームズは私に家に帰るよう勧めた。「だが夜になったら君の助けが必要だ」

「何時だ?」

「10時なら十分だろう」

「ではベーカー街で10時に」

「いいだろう。だがドクター、危険かもしれないから、銃をポケットに入れておいてくれよ」

I could not begin to understand what our business was that night. Where were we going, and what were we going to do? I couldn't understand anything although I had seen and heard every piece of evidence that Holmes had.

When I reached his rooms later that night, he was talking loudly with two men. One I recognized as a policeman.

"Ha! Our party is complete. Watson, let me introduce our guest from Scotland Yard. He is going to join us tonight."

I looked at the Mr. Merryweather whom Holmes introduced. He looked disagreeable and then said, "I am very sorry to be here tonight. I want you to know this is the first Saturday night in twenty-seven years that I have not played a game of rubber with my friends."

"I think you will find the game tonight more exciting," Holmes assured him. "We are looking for the most important head of crime in England."

"John Clay," the policeman said. "He is young but very clever and has been educated at Eton and Oxford. I've been looking for him for years but have never seen him yet. I hope you are right about tonight, Holmes."

"You two go in the first cab," Holmes said. "Watson and I will follow."

■ evidence 图 証拠　■ recognize 動 〜だと分かる　■ party 图 関係者、参加者　■ complete 形 全部そろった　■ Scotland Yard スコットランド・ヤード、ロンドン警視庁　■ disagreeable 形 気難しい、付き合いにくい　■ rubber 图 （ブリッジの）三番勝負《トランプ》　■ assure 動 〜であることを請け合う　■ look for 〜を探す　■ head of 〜のトップ　■ Eton 图 イートン校《イギリスの名門校》

　今夜の仕事がどんなものか、見当もつかなかった。どこへ行き、何をするのか？　ホームズが手にしている証拠は全て私も見聞きしたはずだが、何もわからない。

　夜になってベーカー街の部屋へ行くと、ホームズは二人の男と大声で喋っていた。一人は見覚えのある警官だった。
　「やあ、これで全員そろったな。ワトソン君、こちらはスコットランド・ヤードからの招待客で、今夜の冒険に参加される方だ」
　ホームズが紹介したメリーウェザー氏は、いかにも頑固そうな人物で、こう言った。「今夜皆さんとここにいるのは大変残念だ。この27年間に友人とのブリッジの三番勝負（ラバー）を欠かしたのはこの土曜日が初めてだということを皆さんにも知ってもらいたいものです」

　「こちらのゲームの方が余程エキサイティングだとお分かりになりますよ」ホームズは保証した。「イングランド一の悪党を見つけるのですからね」

　「ジョン・クレイか」警官は言った。「若いが非常に頭が切れて、イートン校とオックスフォード大卒ときてる。長年、奴を追ってるが、お目にかかったことすらないんだ。今晩はあなたが正しいことを祈るばかりですよ、ホームズさん」
　「きみたち二人が前の馬車に乗ってくれれば、ぼくとワトソン君は次の馬車で追いかけるよ」と、ホームズ。

Holmes was in a good mood during the drive. He kept singing over songs which we had heard at the concert that afternoon. Then he explained to me why he brought the two men. "Merryweather is personally interested in this case. Jones is brave and will not let a criminal loose once he has caught him."

We came to our location and sent the cabs away. Mr. Merryweather showed us down a narrow street, winding stone steps and into a large underground room filled with large boxes.

"A strong room," Holmes said.

"Yes," Merryweather said, hitting his stick on the floor. "Why, it sounds quite empty," he said, looking up in surprise.

"I must ask you to be quiet, Mr. Merryweather. Please sit down and be still."

Holmes got down on the floor and began looking at the cracks between the stones. After a few minutes, he jumped up. "We have to wait an hour. After the pawnbroker has gone to bed, they will work fast. Watson, you must know that we are in the basement of one of the largest banks in London. Merryweather is an important man at this bank. He will explain why criminals are interested in this place."

■ sing over ～を繰り返し歌う ■ criminal 图 犯罪者 ■ loose 動 解き放す ■ location 图 場所、位置 ■ winding 形 曲がりくねった ■ strong room 金庫室 ■ empty 形 中身のない、空の ■ look up 見上げる ■ still 形 じっとした、動かない ■ get down 身をかがめる、ひざまずく ■ crack 图 割れ目 ■ basement 图 地階、地下室

　辻馬車で移動する間中、ホームズは上機嫌で、午後のコンサートで聞いたメロディーをずっと口ずさんでいた。そして、二人の男を同道する理由を説明してくれた。「メリーウェザーは個人的にこの事件に関心があるんだ。ジョーンズ警官は勇敢で、犯罪者を一度捕まえたら絶対に逃がさない」

　目的地に着いて、辻馬車を去らせた。メリーウェザー氏が先導して狭い道を抜け、くねる石の階段を降りて、大型の箱で満杯の大きな地下室に入った。

　「金庫室だ」ホームズが言った。
　「その通り」ステッキで床を打ちながら、メリーウェザーが言った。「おや、どうしたんだ、うつろな音がするじゃないか」驚いたように見上げて、彼が言った。
　「お静かに願います、メリーウェザーさん。腰掛けてじっとしていてください」
　ホームズは床に伏して、床石の割れ目を調べ始めた。数分後、ホームズは飛び上がった。「一時間待たねばなりません。質屋が眠りについたら、奴らはスピードを上げるでしょう。ワトソン、ここはロンドンでも有数の銀行の地下室だということに気がついているだろうな。メリーウェザー氏はこの銀行の大物なんだよ。犯罪者がどうしてここに興味を持つのか説明してくださる」

"It is our French gold," Merryweather whispered to me. "Some months ago we were able to buy 30,000 napoleons from the Bank of France. It is known that the money is still in boxes."

"We will have to sit in the dark, now." Holmes told us. "I brought along some cards, hoping that you could still have your game tonight. But it is too dangerous to keep the room lit. When they come, Watson, if they open fire, you must shoot them down."

The dark room was heavy with feeling as we waited for the criminals to come.

"There is only one way of escape. I hope you did as I told you, Jones," Holmes said.

"I sent a chief and two officers to the front door of the house."

"Then we have stopped all the holes. Now we can only wait."

What a wait. It seemed that the whole night passed, but it was only a little more than an hour, I learned later. Suddenly, my eyes caught some light. First it was a spot, then it became a yellow line, then a hand came out of the floor, and went back in again. All was quiet. Soon some stones were thrown aside and a boyish face looked into the room. One knee lifted the body's weight. His companion followed him. He had very red hair.

"It's all clear. Have you got the bags, Archie? Jump!"

"It's no use, John Clay," said Holmes quietly. "You have no chance."

■ French gold フランス金貨　■ whisper 動 ささやく　■ napoleon 图 ナポレオン金貨　■ bring along 携えて来る　■ card 图 トランプのカード　■ keep ～ lit ～を明るくしておく　■ open fire 発砲を開始する　■ shoot down 撃ち殺す　■ chief 图 警部

「フランス金貨だ」メリーウェザー氏は私に耳打ちした。「数ヵ月前、フランス銀行からナポレオン金貨三万枚を購入したのだ。金貨がまだ箱詰めのままであることはよく知られている」

「今から、暗闇の中で座っていなければなりませんよ」ホームズが言った。「あなたがブリッジができるようにと思ってトランプを持参しましたが、明かりをつけておくのは危険すぎる。ワトソン、奴らが来て、もし発砲したら、打ち倒してくれたまえよ」

犯罪者どもが来るのを待つ間、暗い部屋には様々な思いが交錯していた。

「逃げ道は一つしかない。頼んだ通り手配してくれただろうね、ジョーンズ警官」ホームズは言った。

「警部と巡査二名を家の正面玄関に張り付かせました」

「では抜け穴は全て塞いだことになる。今は待つのみだ」

なんという待ち時間だったろう。丸一晩が過ぎたように思えたが、あとで聞くと、たった一時間だった。突然、明かりが見えた。最初は一点だけだったのが、光の筋になり、次いで床から手が出てのびて、また引っ込んだ。すべてが静かだった。まもなく幾つか石が放り出されて、童顔が部屋をのぞいた。片膝に体重をかけて、穴から這い出てきた。相棒が続いたが、濃い赤毛だった。

「問題なしだ。袋は持ったか、アーチー？　飛び込むんだ!」

「無駄だよ、ジョン・クレイ」ホームズが静かに言った。「八方塞がりさ」

■ officer 图 巡査　■ hole 图 穴　■ spot 图 小さな点　■ come out of 〜から出てくる　■ aside 副 わきへ　■ lift 動 持ち上げる　■ companion 图 仲間　■ It'll all clear.「邪魔物はない」　■ be no use 全く役に立たない

"So I see, although you are only holding my pal by his coat."

"There are three men waiting for him at the door."

"How clever you are. I must compliment you."

"And I, you. Your red-headed idea was new and effective."

"I have kings and queens in my family. May I ask you to address me as "Sir" and to say "Please?"

"All right," said Jones, laughing. "Will your Highness please march upstairs so we can take you to prison."

"That is better," said John Clay and walked off to the police car.

"Really, Mr. Holmes," said Mr. Merryweather. "I don't know how the bank can thank you or repay you. You have defeated one of the biggest bank robberies that I have ever heard of."

"I had my own complaints with John Clay and I am glad he has been brought to the law at last. The story told by Mr. Wilson was also most interesting."

Later that night, Holmes explained the mystery to me. "I could see that the criminals only wanted to get the simple pawnbroker out of the way for a few hours every day. The whole plan was drawn up by John Clay. His friend was the man interviewing the red-headed men. As soon as I heard that the assistant was working for half-wages, I thought he must have a reason."

"But how could you guess what his plan was?"

■ pal 图 相棒、仲間　■ compliment 動 ～に賛辞を述べる　■ address 動 (人を～と)呼ぶ　■ Highness 图 殿下　■ prison 图 刑務所　■ walk off 立ち去る　■ repay 動 ～に報いる　■ defeat 動 (敵を)打ち倒す　■ bank robbery 銀行強盗　■ complaint 图 苦情　■ the law 司法当局、警察　■ at last ついに　■ draw up (計画などを)練る　■ guess 動 解きあてる

「そのようだな。もっとも、相棒の方はコートの裾をつかまえただけだがな」

「ドアのところに三人張ってるんだ」

「なんと切れることよ。賛辞を贈るぞ」

「そちらこそ。赤毛の思いつきは斬新で効果的だったからな」

「俺の一族には王や女王がいるんだ。『サー』の称号で呼んでもらおうか。それに『プリーズ』をつけてくれたまえ」

「よし来た」笑いながらジョーンズ警官は言った。「殿下、階段をプリーズ、お上がりあそばして、刑務所へ連行されていただけますかな?」

「それで良し」ジョン・クレイは言って、警察馬車の方へ歩いて行った。

「いや、本当に、ホームズさん」メリーウェザー氏が言った。「当行がどうやって貴殿に感謝できるか、いや報いることができるのか、想像もつきません。史上最大の銀行強盗を阻止してくださった」

「ジョン・クレイには私も個人的に苦情がありましてね、遂に法に裁かれることになって良かった。ウィルソン氏の話も非常に興味深かった」

その夜遅く、ホームズはこのミステリーを説明してくれた。「犯罪者どもが、頭の単純な質屋を毎日数時間だけ店から出したいのだというのは分かった。計画の全容を企てたのはジョン・クレイだ。相棒の方が、赤毛の男たちの面接をしていた奴だ。半値でアシスタントが働いていると聞いた途端、何か裏があると思った」

「だが奴の計画がどうしてわかったんだい?」

"When I heard that he spent hours in the basement, then I thought he must be running a tunnel to another building. When I went to the door of the pawnshop, I saw the knees of his trousers. You must have noticed how dark they were from digging in the earth. Then in our walk on the surrounding streets, I saw the bank nearby. After the concert, I called Scotland Yard and the bank director. That is why the two gentlemen came with us."

"But how did you know they would try the crime tonight?"

"Well, this morning they put the sign on the door. They did not care if Mr. Wilson was in his store or not. That meant they had completed their tunnel. But they had to use it as soon as possible, before the gold was moved. Saturday would be best because they had two days when the bank was closed. For these reasons, I expected them tonight."

"Your reasoning is wonderful," I exclaimed.

"It saves me from boredom," he answered, yawning.

"Do you live to help mankind?"

He moved his shoulders. "Well, maybe it is of some little use. *'L'homme c'est rien—l'oeuvre c'est tout,'* as Gustave Flaubert wrote to George Sand."

■ run a tunnel トンネルを通す　■ notice 動 気が付く　■ dark 形 黒ずんだ　■ dig 動 掘る　■ nearby 副 すぐ近くに　■ bank director 銀行の重役　■ complete 形 完成した　■ exclaim 動 叫ぶ　■ boredom 名 退屈　■ L'homme c'est rien—l'oeuvre c'est tout "The man is nothing—the work is all"　■ Gustave Flaubert ギュスターヴ・フローベール《フランスの小説家、代表作『ボヴァリー夫人』、1821–1880》　■ George Sand ジョルジュ・サンド《フランスの女流作家、1804–1876》

「地下室で何時間も過ごすと聞いた時、別の建物へのトンネルを掘っているのだと考えた。質屋を訪ねたとき、奴のズボンの膝を見たのさ。土を掘るので、真っ黒に汚れていたのに君も気がついたろう？　その後、付近の通りを歩き回って、すぐそばに銀行があるのがわかった。コンサート後に、スコットランド・ヤードと銀行頭取に電話をしたのさ。それであの二人が同行することになったのだ」

「今夜決行するというのは何故わかった？」
「赤毛組合解散の張り紙が今朝出ていたからさ。ウィルソンが店にいようがいまいが、もうどうでも良かったんだ。それはつまり、トンネルが完成したという事だ。しかも金貨が移されてしまう前に、できるだけ早く決行する必要があったんだよ。土曜日なら、銀行が二日間閉まるのだから、最適だ。こういう理由から、今晩だと思ったのさ」

「君の推理は素晴らしいよ」私は叫んだ。
「退屈しのぎにはなるね」ホームズはあくびしながら答えた。
「人類を助けるという使命感を持って生きているのだね？」
　ホームズは肩をすくめた。「恐らく、多少の役には立つだろう。ギュスターヴ・フローベールがジョルジュ・サンドに書き送ったとおりさ。『人間は無——仕事こそ全て』」

覚えておきたい英語表現

> life itself has the most unusual situations, more daring than we can even imagine.（p.52, 9行目）
>
> 人生そのものの方が、最も奇異で、我々の想像を超える大胆な状況をはらんでいるものだと。

【解説】unusualは、「普通じゃない、奇異な」の意味です。良い、悪い、ヘンだとかの価値判断を下さない、オトナの表現です。eventful life（波乱万丈の人生）は、unusualなevents（出来事）も満載で、はらはらドキドキの連続です。あなたも恐れずに、人生のドラマを楽しみましょう！

【例文】① Be daring and take risks! What have you got to lose?
　　　　大胆不敵に、リスクをとれ！ 失うものなんかない。

　　　② He had the most unusual smile when he said good bye.
　　　　お別れを言うとき、彼は見たことがない笑みを浮かべていた。

> What does it mean?（p.58, 6行目）
>
> これはどういうことです？

【解説】meanは、「意味する」という意味です。日本語で「どういうこと？」は、英語では、「どういう意味？」と言います。言葉や事柄の意味がわからないので、説明を求めているのです。

【例文】① I don't understand what you mean. Please explain to me once more.
　　　　あなたが言っていることがわかりません。もう一度説明してくれませんか。

　　　② I really mean it!
　　　　真剣に言っています！　　＊すでに述べたことを強調する際に使う表現です。

> Holmes laughed with pleasure.（p.58, 7行目）
>
> ホームズは嬉しそうに笑った。

【解説】with pleasureは、「うれしそうに、よろこんで」の意味です。
Thank you!（ありがとう）と言われたら、With pleasure!（よろこんで！）と、にっこり笑って返答することができます。

【例文】① I would accept the work with pleasure.
喜んでお仕事をお引き受けいたします。

② Her face lit up with pleasure when she saw her grandson for the first time.
孫の顔を初めて見たとき、彼女の顔は喜びで輝いた。

He was happy to have a day off work.（p.62, 9行目）
やつは一日仕事を休めて嬉しそうでした。

【解説】to have a day offは、「一日休みを取る」の意味です。

【例文】① I want to request to have a day off tomorrow.
明日一日お休みをいただきたいのですが。

② She was happy to have a day off to spend with her children.
彼女は一日休暇を取って子供たちと一緒に過ごすことができてうれしかった。

It was hard to believe they were so close.（p.76, 2行目）
こんな目と鼻の先にあるとは信じがたい。

【解説】hard to believe ～は、「～が信じがたい」という意味です。 closeは、「クロース」と発音し、「近い」という意味です。物理的・心理的距離の近さを表わします。

【例文】① It's hard to believe that you are here with me now.
今、君がこうして僕と一緒にいるなんて、信じられないよ。

② We are close, yet so far…
私たちは近くにいても、心は離れてしまった…

Holmes was in a good mood during the drive.（p.80, 1行目）
(辻馬車で) 移動する間中、ホームズは上機嫌だった。

【解説】in a good moodは、「上機嫌」という意味です。

【例文】I'm sorry I'm not in a good mood today.
悪いけど、今日は虫の居所が悪いんだ。

THE
ADVENTURE
SPECKLED
BAND

なんと朝の7時15分にホームズとワトソンは、
恐怖にふるえ、取り乱した若い女性の訪問をうける。
彼女の姉は2年前に不審な死をとげたのだが、そのとき
低い口笛が聞こえた。それと同じ口笛がまた聞こえたので、
夜が明けるのを待ちかねて相談に来たのだった。
ホームズの行動は早かった。その日の夜には彼女の寝室にワトソンと
ふたりでひそみ、暗闇のなかでジッと何かが起こるのを待つ……

この殺人方法には無理があるのではないかという指摘はあるものの、
ドイル自身がいちばん気に入っていて、またファンのあいだでも
ダントツの人気を誇る作品。短編としては8作目で、
ホームズ物語の面白さがいろいろな面で最高潮に達している。

OF THE まだらの紐

The Adventure of the Speckled Band

I have worked with Sherlock Holmes on more than seventy cases in the last eight years. Some were sad, some funny, many only strange, but none ordinary. He always worked for the love of his art rather than for money. However, the most unusual was the case of the Roylott family of Stoke Moran. The case happened when we were both still living on Baker Street. I may have recorded them earlier, but I had to keep many of the facts secret until now. Within the last month, the lady to whom I promised secrecy has died and I think it is best that I bring the secret to light. The rumors about this case are worse than the truth.

It was early in April of 1883 when I found Sherlock Holmes standing next to my bed waiting for me to wake up, though it was still seven o'clock in the morning and he was usually a late sleeper.

■ speckled 形 たくさんの小さな斑点のついた　■ may have p.p. ～したかもしれない
■ secrecy 名 秘密にしていること　■ bring ～ to light ～を明るみに出す、公にする
■ rumor 名 うわさ、風説　■ wake up 目を覚ます　■ late sleeper 朝寝ぼうの人

まだらの紐

　シャーロック・ホームズとは、この8年で70件以上の事件にあたってきた。悲しいもの、滑稽なもの、ただ奇妙に尽きるものと様々だが、ありきたりのものは一つとして無い。ホームズは常に、金のためではなく、己の手腕を発揮できる仕事を愛したのだ。しかしながら、最も異色なのは、ストーク・モーランのロイロット家の事件だろう。この事件は、我々が二人共、まだベーカー街に住んでいた頃に起きた。既に事件簿には記してあるものの、現在までは多くの事実関係を秘密にしておかなければならなかった。先月、我々が守秘を誓った当事者の女性が亡くなり、秘密を明るみに出すことがベストと考えた。この事件にまつわる巷の噂が、事実よりも醜悪なものであるからだ。

　あれは1883年4月初旬のこと、枕元でシャーロック・ホームズが立って私が起きるのを待っているのに気がついた。まだ午前7時で、ホームズは朝は遅いタイプだったにもかかわらずだ。

"Very sorry to wake you up so early, Watson."

"What? Is there a fire?"

"No, a young lady who needs to see me. When young ladies wake people up early in the morning, I think there must be something very important to talk about. I thought you would like to listen from the beginning, so I am calling you to give you the chance."

"My dear fellow, I would not miss it for anything," I replied, getting up and quickly dressing.

There was no greater pleasure than following Holmes in his work and admiring his quick mind and intuition. The young lady was dressed in black and had a veil over her face. When we entered the room, she stood up.

"Good morning, madam," said Holmes cheerfully. "My name is Sherlock Holmes. This is my close friend, Dr. Watson. You may speak as freely before him as before myself. Oh, I see that you are shivering. Come close to the fire."

"It is not cold which makes me shiver. It is fear, Mr. Holmes. It is terror."

She removed the veil from her face and we could see that her face was pale, with frightened eyes. She looked like a hunted animal. She seemed to be about thirty years old, but she looked even older. Holmes ran his eyes over her, seeing so much.

■ fellow 名 仲間、同志　■ My dear fellow.「ねえ、君」　■ admire 動 ～を称賛する
■ intuition 名 直感（力）　■ veil 名（女性が顔を覆う網の）ベール　■ shiver 動 震える
■ pale 形 青ざめた　■ frightened 動 脅えた　■ hunted 形 追われた

「こんなに早く起こして申し訳ない、ワトソン君」

「なんだ？ 火事か？」

「いや、若い女性の面会だ。若い女性が早朝に人を起こすからには、非常に重要な話だと思うのだ。君も最初から聞きたいだろうと思ってね、チャンスを与えているわけだ」

「君、何があっても逃すものか」起きて素早く着替えながら言った。

ホームズの仕事に付き添って、彼の頭の素早い回転ぶりとカンを鑑賞するくらい、面白いことはない。当の若い女性は黒い服をまとい、ベールで顔を覆っていた。我々が入っていくと立ち上がった。

「お早うございます、マダム」ホームズは朗らかに言った。「私がシャーロック・ホームズです。こちらは親友のワトソン博士。彼の前では、私に対すると同じように自由にお話しいただいて構いません。おや、震えていらっしゃいますね。もっと火のそばへ」

「震えているのは、寒さのせいではございません。恐れのためでございます、ホームズさま。恐怖のためなのでございます」

ベールを外すと、青ざめ、恐怖におののいた眼をしているのがわかった。追われる動物のようであった。年は30ほどであろうが、さらに老けて見える。ホームズは彼女を素早く観察して多くを見て取った。

"You must not fear," he said kindly, touching her arm. "We will make everything all right. I see that you have just arrived by train."

"You know me?"

"No, but I see the half of a return ticket in your glove. You must have left home very early and traveled by dog-cart to the train station."

She looked shocked.

"There is no surprise. Your coat is covered with spots of mud in seven places. Only a dog-cart could make mud come like that on your coat."

"Whatever way you have of finding out, you are quite right," said she. "I left home before six this morning and got the first train to Waterloo. Sir, I cannot be like this any longer. There is only one person who cares for me and he cannot help. I have heard of you, Mr. Holmes, from my friend, Mrs. Farintosh. She said that you help people in their hour of need, and it is from her that I have received your address. Please try to throw a little light on the darkness which surrounds me. I cannot reward you now, but in six weeks I shall be married, with my own income, and I will show you how grateful I am then."

■ make everything all right すべてうまくいく　■ return ticket 往復切符　■ dog-cart 图 二輪馬車　■ spot 图 染み　■ whatever 厖 どんな〜でも　■ Waterloo 图 ウォータールー駅　■ like this このように　■ any longer これ以上　■ hour of need 助けが必要なとき　■ reward 動 〜に報酬を与える　■ income 图 所得、収入　■ grateful 厖 感謝する

「恐れてはいけない」ホームズは、彼女の腕に触れながら優しく言った。
「我々がすべてを上手く収めましょう。列車で着かれたばかりなのですね」

「わたくしのことをご存知なのですか」
「いいえ、しかし手袋をした手に往復切符の半券を握りしめていらっしゃいますね。今朝、非常に早く家を出て、二輪馬車で駅まで行かれたのでしょう」

女性はショックを受けたようであった。
「驚くことはありませんよ。外套に泥ハネが七箇所、付いている。そんな風に泥を跳ね上げるのは、二輪馬車だけですよ」

「どういう方法でお知りになったとしても、おっしゃる通りでございます」女性は言った。「今朝6時前に家を出まして、ウォータールー駅までの始発に乗りました。ホームズさま、このままではもう、やって参ることができません。私のことを気にかけてくれるのはたったひとりでして、その彼も助けにはなれないのです。あなた様のことは、ホームズさま、友人のファリントッシュ夫人から聞き及んでおりました。困っている人を助けてくださる方であると。あなたさまの御住所も夫人から伺ったのでございます。私を取り巻く闇に、わずかでも光を投げかけてくださいませ。今、御礼を差し上げることはできませんが、6週間しましたら結婚し、自分の収入が得られることになっております。その折には私の感謝の気持ちをお示しいたします」

Holmes unlocked his desk and took out a notebook.

"Farintosh," said he. "Ah, yes, I remember. A white opal necklace. I shall be happy to devote as much attention to you as I did to your friend. About payment, my job is my payment. You may cover my expenses as you please. Now please give us the information that will make it possible to help you."

"Oh," she cried. "My fears are based on such small matters. Even that one person who could help me thinks that my problems are only in my own mind. But I believe that you, Mr. Holmes, can see deeply into the unkind human heart. You will be able to tell me how to walk through the dangers I face."

"I will try, madam."

"My name is Helen Stoner. I am living with my stepfather, the oldest member of the Saxon family in England. We were once the richest family in England, but my grandfather, and his father before him wasted our money, so that now we only have a two-hundred-year-old house with a heavy mortgage. My stepfather trained as a doctor and worked in India. After many robberies, he got angry and beat his Indian servant. He was sent to prison and years later returned to England a very unhappy man.

■ unlock 動 ～を開錠する　■ opal 图 オパール《宝石》　■ devote 動（時間や注意など を）充てる　■ expense 图 経費　■ be based on ～に基づいている　■ unkind 厖 冷酷な ■ face 動 ～に直面する　■ stepfather 图 義父　■ Saxon 图 サクソン人　■ mortgage 图 抵当　■ train 動 訓練を受ける

ホームズは机の鍵を開けて、ノートを取り出した。

「ファリントッシュ夫人……ああ、そうだ、思い出した。白のオパールのネックレス。ご友人の事件にかけたのと同じ注意力を傾けて、あなたのケースにも当たりましょう。お支払いですが、私にとっては仕事が報酬なのです。お望みなら経費をカバーしていただきましょう。ではお力になれるよう、詳細を話してください」

「ああ」女性は叫んだ。「私の恐れというのは、ごく些細な事柄に根ざしているのでございます。わたくしのことを助けてくれるたったひとりの人さえ、わたくしの思い込みだと考えているのでございます。でもわたくしは、ホームズさま、あなた様なら冷酷な人間の心の底までお見通しであると信じております。どうやったらこの危険をすりぬけていくことができるか、教えてくださるはずでございます」

「そのように努めましょう」

「わたくしはヘレン・ストーナーと申します。同居している義理の父は、サクソン系イングランド人の中で最も由緒ある家の出でございます。一時はイングランドで最も裕福な家柄でしたが、祖父と曽祖父が浪費を重ねまして、現在は重い抵当に入っている築200年の古い館が残るのみでございます。義父は医学を学び、インドで仕事についておりましたが、頻繁に強盗が入ることに腹を立て、ある日、インド人の使用人を殴りました。刑務所行きとなり、何年もしてから失意のうちに、気難しい人間となってイングランドに戻ったのでございます。

"It was later that my mother married our stepfather; she gave all of her money to him, about 1,000 pounds a year, with a note that some of the money would go to me and my sister at our marriage. My mother died about eight years ago in a train accident, but we had enough money to live comfortably with him. At her death, he took us to live in his family house in the country. My sister and I were twins, so we were always very close and enjoyed each other's company very much there.

"But my stepfather often became very angry. He started to fight with everyone. Twice the police had to come into our house, the fighting was so bad. He was very strong and we were all afraid of him.

"Last week, he hurt a man badly and I had to give him all the money I had to keep him quiet. My stepfather had no friends except the wandering gypsies. Sometimes they came to live on our land in their tents, and other times he even left our home to travel with the gypsies.

"You can understand that my sister and I had little happiness. No servant would stay in our house. We did all the work. Finally, my sister, though she was only thirty years old, died. Her hair was already completely white."

"Your sister is dead, then?"

■ accident 图 事故 ■ comfortably 副 楽に ■ twins 图 双子 ■ enjoy each other's company 和気あいあいと楽しむ ■ hurt 動 ～を傷つける ■ keep someone quiet (人)の口を封じる ■ wandering 形 さすらう ■ gypsy 图 ジプシー、ロマ民族の人

100

　母とはその後で結婚いたしました。母は、年に1000ポンドほどあった収入すべてを父に与え、その一部は私と姉が結婚した時にそれぞれに与えると取り決めたのでございます。母は8年前、鉄道事故で亡くなりましたが、私たちは義父と一緒に快適に暮らせるだけの余裕がございました。母の死後、義父は姉と私を連れ、自分の先祖伝来の館に住むことにいたしました。姉と私は双子でしたので、非常に仲が良く、その館でもずっと一緒に過ごしました。

　しかし義父は、頻繁に激高するようになりまして、誰とでも喧嘩をするようになりました。喧嘩があまりひどいため、警察が館の中まで入ったことも二度ございます。義父は腕っ節が非常に強く、私たちは皆、義父を恐れておりました。
　先週のこと、義父がある男に大怪我をさせまして、私はありったけのお金を与えて男を黙らせなければなりませんでした。義父には、流浪のジプシー以外には友人がおりません。ジプシー達が所有地にテントを張って住み着いたり、義父が彼らと旅に出てしまうことすらございます。

　姉と私にとっていかにつらい状況であったか、ご理解いただけるかと存じます。使用人は誰ひとりとして居着かず、私たちがすべてをこなしておりました。ついに姉が、たった30歳で亡くなりました。髪の毛は真っ白でございました」
　「姉上は既に亡くなられたのですね?」

"She died two years ago. That is what I have come to talk to you about. We had few friends. Occasionally we went to see my mother's sister near Harrow. Julia went there at Christmas two years ago and met a man with whom she became engaged to marry. My father heard of the wedding plans and did not seem displeased. But just before the wedding took place, I lost her."

Until this time, Holmes had had his eyes closed. But at this point, he opened them slightly and looked at his visitor.

"Please explain the details."

"Oh, I can forget none of them. Our house is old, as I said. We lived in only one side of it. There were sitting rooms and then the bedrooms. My father's bedroom was first, my sister's second, and mine, the third. All the doors open into the same hallway."

"I see."

"The windows of the three rooms open out onto a green grassy area. That night, my father had gone to his bedroom early, but my sister could smell cigars which she did not like, from his room, so she came into my room. We talked for a long time about her upcoming wedding, then she stood up to go.

" 'Tell me, Helen,' she said, 'have you ever heard anyone whistle in the dead of the night?'

" 'Never,' I said.

■ occasionally 副 時折　■ become engaged to ～と婚約する　■ displeased 形 気を悪くさせられた　■ take place 行われる、開催される　■ detail 名 詳細　■ none 代 何も～ない　■ open into ～の方へ通じる　■ hallway 名 廊下　■ open out onto ～に向けて開く　■ grassy 形 草の生い茂った　■ cigar 名 葉巻　■ upcoming 形 もうすぐやって来る　■ Have you ever ～? ～したことがありますか　■ whistle 動 笛[口笛]を吹く

「2年前でございました。このことをお話しに参ったのです。私たちは友人も少ないのですが、時々はハロウに住む母方の叔母に会いに行っておりました。姉のジュリアは2年前のクリスマスに訪れた折、ある男性と出会い、婚約いたしました。父も結婚の計画を聞いて、反対ではないようでございました。ですが、式の直前になって姉が亡くなったのでございます」

それまで眼を閉じて聞いていたホームズが、この時点で薄目を開け、訪問者の女性を見つめた。

「もっと細かくお話しください」

「どの細部も、忘れられるものではございません。館は、先ほど申しましたとおり、古いものでして、私たちは片翼だけ使用しております。居間と寝室がございまして、父の寝室がまずあり、姉のが2番目、私のが3番目となっております。どの寝室も、ドアは同じ廊下に開くようになっております」

「なるほど」

「3つの寝室の窓は、草の茂った緑地に面しております。あの夜、父は早めに寝室に引き取りましたが、父の寝室から葉巻の嫌な匂いがするからと言って、姉は私の寝室に参りました。来る結婚式について長いこと話し合ってから、姉は立ち上がって行きかけました。

『ねえヘレン』姉は申しました。『真夜中に誰かが口笛を吹くのを聞いたことがある?』

『全然ないわ』私は答えました。

" 'I suppose that you could not whistle in your sleep?'

" 'Of course not.'

" 'The last few nights, about three o'clock in the morning, I hear someone whistling. It wakes me up. I thought maybe you had heard it, too.'

" 'No, it must be the gypsies living on our land.'

" 'Yes, maybe.' And she went into her room and turned the lock."

"Did you always lock your doors at night?" Holmes asked her.

"Yes, of course."

"I could not sleep that night. Our souls were so close, being twins. It was raining, and then there was a wild scream of a frightened woman. I knew that it was my sister's voice. I ran from my bed. I heard a whistle, as she had described and then some metal fell. I ran down the hall to my sister's door. It was open. Then my sister appeared in the doorway. Her face was white and her body was shaking. I ran to her and held her in my arms, but she fell to the ground. She looked so strange, but she knew me and said, 'Oh, my God! Helen! It was the band! The speckled band!' She tried to say something else, but could not. She pointed to our father's room, then she was gone. My father came running from his room and tried to help her, but it was too late. That was the end of my dearest sister."

■ maybe 副 もしかすると　■ scream 名 悲鳴　■ describe 動 ～を言い表す　■ metal 名 金属　■ appear 動 現れる　■ band 名 ひも、ベルト　■ gone 形 （人が）死んだ

『寝言で口笛を吹くなんて、あり得ないわよね?』

『もちろんないわよ』

『ここ何晩か、午前3時頃に誰かの口笛が聞こえるのよ。それで目が覚めるの。あなたも聞いたかと思ったんだけど』

『ここに住み着いているジプシーに違いないわ』

『そうね、そうかもしれないわね』そうして姉は自分の寝室に戻り、鍵をかけました」

「あなた方は、夜いつもドアに鍵をかけるのですか?」ホームズは尋ねた。

「もちろんでございます」

「私はその晩、眠れませんでした。双子というのは、魂の結びつきが非常に強いものでございます。雨が降っておりましたが、恐怖に満ちた女性の叫び声が聞こえました。姉の声であるとわかりました。ベッドから飛び出すと、姉が申しておりました通りの口笛が聞こえ、それから金属の落ちるような音がいたしました。廊下をかけて姉の部屋に参りましたら、ドアは開いており、姉が出てきました。蒼白で全身を震わせておりました。かけつけて抱きしめましたが、姉はくずれおちてしまいました。全く我を忘れたような様子でも、私のことは分かりまして、申しました。『なんてこと! ヘレン! 紐だったのよ! まだらの紐よ!』姉はもっと言おうとしましたが、できませんでした。父の寝室を指差し、そして息を引き取ったのでございます。父も寝室から走り出て来て、姉を助けようといたしましたが、遅すぎました。これが大切な姉の最期の様子でございます」

"One moment," said Holmes, "are you sure about this whistle and metallic sound?"

"That is what the coroner asked me. Well, I think I heard it but there was such a terrible storm, maybe it was in my head."

"Was your sister in her clothes?"

"No, in her bedclothes. And in her right hand was a match, and in her left a matchbox."

"So she was lighting a match when the accident happened. What did the coroner say?"

"He could not find any cause for death. I know that the door and the windows were locked. The walls were solid and so were the floors. It is certain that my sister was alone when she met her end. Besides, there were no marks of any violence upon her."

"How about poison?"

"The doctors could find nothing."

"Then what did she die of?"

"Of fear and nervous shock, but I don't know what frightened her."

"Were there gypsies on your land then?"

"Yes, there are almost always some there."

"What do you understand from the 'speckled band' she spoke of?"

■ metallic 形 金属性の　■ coroner 名 検死官　■ in one's clothes 洋服を着たまま [着替えずに]　■ bedclothes 名 寝まき　■ match 名 マッチ (棒)　■ matchbox 名 マッチ箱　■ light a match マッチに火を付ける　■ solid 形 頑丈な　■ certain 形 明白な　■ besides 副 その上　■ violence 名 暴力　■ poison 名 毒物　■ nervous shock 神経性ショック　■ speak of 〜を口にする

「待ってください」ホームズは言った。「口笛と金属音が聞こえたのは確かですね?」

「検死官にもそのように聞かれました。聞こえたと思ったのですが、外はひどい嵐でしたので、私の思い違いかもしれません」

「姉上は日中の服装のままでしたか?」

「いいえ、寝巻き姿でした。右手にはマッチを、左手にはマッチ箱を握っておりました」

「とすると姉上は、事故が起こったとき、マッチをつけておられたのですね。検死官はなんと言ったのですか」

「死因となるようなものは何も見つけられませんでした。私もドアと窓に鍵がかかっていたことは知っております。壁は頑丈で、床も同じです。姉が最期を迎えたとき、一人だったことは確かなのでございます。加えて、暴力を加えられたような痕は見つかりませんでした」

「毒物はどうですか?」

「検死医たちは何も発見できませんでした」

「では死因はなんだったのですか」

「恐怖と神経ショックでございますが、何がそれほど恐ろしかったのか私にはわからないのでございます」

「ジプシーたちは当時、敷地内にいたのですか」

「はい、いつも何人かがおります」

「姉上の言った『まだらの紐(バンド)』は何のことだと思いますか」

"I never knew. Perhaps a band of people, perhaps a kind of handkerchief."

Holmes shook his head in disagreement.

"Please continue your explanation."

"During the past two years my life has been very lonely. A month ago, a dear friend asked me to marry him. My father is not against our plan. We hope to be married in the spring. We are repairing our house, and two days ago, my room was broken down, so I moved into my sister's bedroom. I was sleeping in her bed last night. Imagine how frightened I was when I heard the whistle which she heard before her death. I lit a lamp, but there was nothing in my room. I got the train first thing this morning to visit you and seek your advice."

"That is good, but have you told me everything?"

"Yes, all."

"Miss Stoner, you have not. You are protecting your father."

"Why, what do you mean?"

Holmes pushed back the arm of her dress and showed black marks from four fingers and one thumb on her arm.

"You have been treated cruelly."

At this, she turned red. "He does not know his own strength."

■ band of ～の一群、～の集団　■ disagreement 图 不一致、相違　■ explanation 图 説明　■ against 前 ～に反対して　■ repair 動 ～を修繕する　■ break down 取り壊す　■ move into（場所や建物に）移る　■ first thing（その日の行動が）最初に　■ seek 動 ～を探し求める　■ protect 動 ～をかばう　■ push back 押しやる　■ cruelly 副 むごく　■ strength 图 力

「全くわからないのでございます。紐というよりもジプシー集団という意味のバンドかもしれず、あるいはハンカチの一種かと思ったりいたします」

ホームズは違うというように頭を振った。

「どうぞお話を続けてください」

「この2年間というもの、私の人生は非常に寂しいものでございましたが、1ヵ月前、親しい友人からプロポーズを受けました。父は私たちの計画に反対しておりません。春には式を挙げたいと考えております。父の館は現在改修中でございまして、2日前、私の寝室が取り壊されましたので、姉の部屋に移りました。昨晩、姉のベッドで休んでおりましたら、姉が死ぬ前に聞いた口笛が聞こえたのでございます。私の恐怖をご想像いただけますでしょうか。ランプをつけましたが、部屋には誰もおりません。朝一番、とにかく列車に飛び乗ってあなた様をお訪ねし、アドバイスを頂きに参ったのでございます」

「それは良かった。だが全てを話していただけましたかな?」

「はい、全て申し上げました」

「ストーナーさん、お話しになっていませんよ。お父上をかばっていらっしゃいますね」

「なぜ、どういうことでございましょう?」

ホームズがストーナー嬢のドレスの腕をまくりあげると、親指と四本指の跡を示す黒いあざがくっきりとついていた。

「過酷な扱いを受けて来られましたね」

ここに来て、ストーナー嬢は赤くなった。「父は自分の強さがわからないのでございます」

Holmes looked into the fire. "There are one thousand details I wish I could know now. But we do not have a moment to lose. If we go to your house immediately, we can see the rooms without your father knowing."

"He will be out of the house all day today. No one is there to disturb you."

"Are you coming, Watson?"

"Of course."

"What are you going to do?" Holmes asked Miss Stoner.

"I have one or two things to do in London, and I will return by the noon train to be there in time for your arrival."

"Then you may expect us in the early afternoon. Will you stay now and join us for breakfast?"

"No, I must go. I feel better now that I have talked to you." She dropped the veil over her face and left the room quietly.

"What do you think, Watson?"

"I cannot guess about this unhappy situation."

"If everything is true, her sister must have been alone when she died."

"But what of the whistles and the strange words of the dying woman?"

"I cannot think."

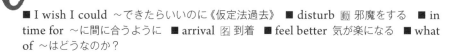

■ I wish I could ～できたらいいのに《仮定法過去》　■ disturb 動 邪魔をする　■ in time for ～に間に合うように　■ arrival 名 到着　■ feel better 気が楽になる　■ what of ～はどうなのか？

ホームズは暖炉の火をみつめた。「今、知りたい細部情報は千もある。しかし、一時も無駄にしてはいられない。我々があなたの家に今すぐ行けば、お父上に知られずに部屋を見られますか」

「父は今日は一日留守でございます。お邪魔をする者はございません」

「君も来るかね、ワトソン君?」
「もちろんだとも」
「あなたはどうされますか」ホームズはストーナー嬢に尋ねた。
「ロンドンで少し用事がございますので、正午の列車で、あなた様がお着きになる前に戻っているようにいたします」
「では午後早い時間に伺いましょう。少しお待ちいただいて、朝食をご一緒にいかがですか」
「いいえ、もう参りませんと。お話しできたことで、気持ちが軽くなりました」ベールを垂らして、ストーナー嬢は静かに出て行った。
「どう思うかね、ワトソン君?」
「この不幸な状況については、何も思いつかんね」
「ストーナー嬢の話が全て本当なら、彼女の姉は死んだときは独りでいたことになる」
「だが、口笛と、彼女が死ぬ前に言った奇妙な言葉はどうなんだ?」

「思いつかない」

"When you think about the old man and his friendliness with the gypsies, it is possible that he wanted to prevent her marriage. The band could be the gypsies, or the metal band on the window. But I cannot understand anything. That is why we are going to visit the house today."

Just then a huge man entered our room. He had on a top-hat, a long coat, and a horse whip in his hand. He was so tall his hat touched the ceiling, and his face looked evil.

"Which of you is Holmes?" he asked.

"I am," Holmes said quietly.

"I am Dr. Roylott, of Stoke Moran."

"I see," said Holmes without any surprise.

"Why has my daughter been here to see you? What did she say to you?" he screamed.

"The flowers are blooming nicely this year, aren't they?" Holmes replied.

"Ha! You scoundrel. I have heard of you. You cause trouble."

My friend smiled.

"Don't you cause any trouble in my life. I am a dangerous man." He picked up a tool for the fire and bent it in half. "See that this does not happen to you." And he left the room.

■ friendliness 图 友好的であること ■ prevent 動 ～を防ぐ ■ top-hat 图 トップ・ハット、シルクハット ■ horse whip 乗馬用むち ■ ceiling 图 天井 ■ evil 形 邪悪な ■ bloom 動 花が咲く ■ scoundrel 图 悪党 ■ cause trouble トラブルを引き起こす ■ tool 图 道具 ■ bent 動 bend (～を曲げる) の過去形 ■ in half 半分に

「父親の性格とジプシー達との交流を考えると、ストーナー嬢の結婚を阻止したいと思っても不思議はない。紐というのはジプシーのことか、あるいは金属の窓枠かもしれない。だが何も筋が通らん。だから今日、家を見に行くんだ」

ちょうどその時、大男が部屋に踏み込んできた。トップハットに長い外套、馬の鞭を手にしている。あまりに背が高いので、トップハットが天井に付くようで、顔つきは邪悪だった。
「どちらがホームズだ?」男は聞いた。
「私だ」ホームズは静かに答えた。
「ストーク・モランのドクター・ロイロットだ」
「そうか」ホームズは平然として答えた。
「娘がお前を訪ねたのは何故だ?　お前に何を言った?」男はわめいた。

「今年の花は美しいと思わないかね?」と、ホームズ。

「は!　この悪党め。お前のことは聞いているぞ。トラブルメーカーだとな」
友はにっこりした。
「俺にはトラブルを起こすなよ。俺は危険な男だからな」男は暖炉用の器具をとって2つに折り曲げた。「お前もこうならないようにしろ」そして出て行った。

"He seems a friendly person," Holmes said, laughing. "Now we will have breakfast, Watson, and then I will go down to the hospital where I will try to get some information to help us before we take the train."

It was almost one o'clock when Holmes returned. He had a blue sheet of paper with a lot of numbers written on it.

"I have seen the will of his late wife. The total income is now only 750 pounds a year, which means that in the case of marriage each daughter can get only 250 pounds. That means that this fine man would have hardly any money if both daughters married. He has the very strongest reasons for preventing the girl marrying. Now, Watson, we must leave immediately. I would be very grateful to you if you would put your gun in your pocket. That and our toothbrushes are, I think, all that we need to take."

We reached the house easily. There was a bright sun, few clouds, and it was a perfect day, in general. There was a strange contrast between the sweet promise of spring and this ugly work we had to do. My friend was resting, lost in deepest thought. Suddenly he touched my shoulder and pointed over the land.

"Look there!" he said.

We could see an old mansion.

"Stoke Moran?" he asked.

■ will 图 遺言状　■ fine 形 すてきな、立派な　■ hardly 副 ほとんど〜ない
■ toothbrush 图 歯ブラシ　■ contrast 图 対比、コントラスト　■ ugly 形 醜い、不快な
■ resting 形 休んでいる　■ be lost in 没頭している　■ mansion 图 館

「愛想がいい奴じゃないか」ホームズは笑いながら言った。「さて朝食にするか、ワトソン君。その後、僕は病院へ行って必要な情報を得てくるとしよう。列車に乗る前にね」

ホームズが戻ったのは1時近かった。数字を一杯書いた青い紙を手にしていた。

「亡くなったロイロット夫人の遺書を見たよ。収入合計は年に750ポンドに減っている。娘たちが結婚時にもらえるのは250ポンドずつしかない。ということは、2人とも結婚したら、奴は手元に金がほとんど残らなくなるということだ。ストーナー嬢の結婚を阻止する最強の動機があるわけだ。さあ、ワトソン、すぐに出発しなければ。君の銃をポケットに忍ばせてくれればありがたい。それと歯ブラシだな、持っていくのはそれだけでいい」

館に行くのは簡単だった。快晴で、雲もほとんど無く、素晴らしい日だったといえる。春の甘い予感と、我々の手がける醜悪な事件とのコントラストが奇妙だった。友は沈思し、静かだった。突然、私の肩を掴むと、指を指した。

「見たまえ!」
古い館が見えた。
「ストーク・モランか?」ホームズは尋ねた。

"Yes, that is it," said the driver. "And the fastest way to get to it is to walk across the fields, as the lady is doing."

"And the lady is Miss Stoner? Yes, we shall do as you say."

We crossed over the stile, and went across the fields toward her. Her face was full of joy when she saw us.

"I am so glad you could come. Dr. Roylott is away, and he will not be back until evening."

"We have already met the good man," Holmes said, explaining the morning event.

"Good heavens! He has followed me then. What shall I do?"

"You must be very careful. If he is mean to you tonight, we shall take you away to your aunt's at Harrow. But now, we must use our time wisely."

The building was old with broken windows covered with wooden boards, and blue smoke curling above into the sky. Some workmen were present. Holmes walked around the old house slowly.

"These are the bedrooms as you described them?"

"Yes."

"Are there windows?"

"Yes, but too small for anyone to pass."

"I see. Please go into your sister's bedroom and close the windows tight."

■ get to ～に着く　■ shall 助 ～しましょうか　■ cross over ～を越える　■ stile 名 踏み段　■ be away 不在で　■ event 名 出来事　■ Good heavens!「まさか」《驚きを表す》　■ mean 形 卑劣な、意地悪な　■ wisely 副 賢明に　■ curl 動 渦巻いて進む　■ present 形 出勤して、居合わせて

「そうでさあ」御者が言った。「一番手っ取り早いのは野原を横切っていくことでさあ、あのご婦人のように」

「あれはストーナー嬢か？　よし、我々も君の言うとおりにしよう」

我々は、石垣の踏み越し段を越えて野原を横切り、ストーナー嬢に近づいた。我々を見た瞬間、彼女の顔は嬉しさで輝いた。

「いらして頂けて、本当に嬉しいですわ。ドクター・ロイロットは不在で、夕方まで戻りませんの」

「素敵なお父上にはもうお会いしましたよ」今朝の出来事をホームズは説明した。

「なんてこと！　私の後をつけたんですわ。どうしましょう？」

「非常に注意深くあることです。今晩、あなたに酷い態度を取るようなら、ハロウの叔母さまの家にお連れしましょう。だが今は、時間を賢く使わねば」

館は古く、破れ窓には板が打ち付けてあり、青い煙が空に立ち上っていた。工事の作業員がいるのだ。ホームズは古い館のまわりをゆっくりと歩き回った。

「こちらがあなたのお話しになった寝室ですね」

「さようでございます」

「窓はありますか」

「はい、でも人が通り抜けられる大きさではございません」

「わかりました。では姉上の寝室に入り、窓をしっかり閉めてください」

Miss Stoner did so. Holmes tried to open the windows but could not. Even a knife could not be passed through. "Hum, I cannot figure out how anyone could enter the room. We must look inside."

It was a nice little room. A small bed and dressing-table. A brown chair and carpet.

"Please excuse me," he said, and he threw himself down on the floor to examine the wood. He examined the walls in the same way. Then he pulled on the rope over the bed, but there was no bell. There was also a hole in the ceiling connecting this room to the stepfather's bedroom.

"This is a very strange rope," Holmes said. "We shall now look at the inner bedroom."

Dr. Roylott's room was larger, but still plainly furnished. There were many books, an armchair beside the bed and a plain wooden chair.

"What's in here?" Holmes asked, touching the safe.

"Only business papers."

"So you have seen inside?"

"Only years ago, there were business papers."

"Not a cat?"

"No, what a strange idea!"

"Well, here is a dish of milk."

■ figure out 見当がつく　■ dressing-table 名 化粧台　■ throw oneself down on the floor 床に寝転ぶ　■ in the same way 同様に　■ rope 名 綱　■ inner 形 （場所が）内部の、内側の　■ plainly 副 質素に、簡素に　■ furnish 動 家具などを備え付ける　■ safe 名 金庫　■ dish 名 皿

118

　ストーナー嬢はそのとおりにした。ホームズは外から窓を開けようとしたが、できなかった。ナイフの刃の入る隙間も無いだろう。「ふうむ、誰かが外から入れるとはとても思えないな。内部を調べなくては」

　中は、小さいが感じの良い部屋だった。小さなベッドと化粧台、茶色の椅子に絨毯が置かれていた。

　「失礼」ホームズは言って、腹ばいになり、床板を調べた。同じように壁も調べた。それからベッドの枕元に垂れ下がっている呼び鈴の引き綱を引っ張ったが、呼び鈴は鳴らなかった。天井にも通風孔の穴があり、隣の父親の寝室とつながっていた。

　「この引き綱は実に奇妙だ」ホームズは言った。「今度は一番奥の寝室を見るとしよう」

　ドクター・ロイロットの寝室はもっと大きかったが、やはり簡素な家具しか置いていなかった。本が沢山と、ベッドの脇に肘掛け椅子、簡素な木の椅子。

　「この中には何が入っているのですか?」ホームズが、金庫に触れながら尋ねた。

　「書類だけでございます」

　「見たことがあるんですね?」

　「何年も前でございますけれど、書類が入っておりました」

　「猫ではなく?」

　「いいえ、どうしてまたそんなことを!」

　「ミルク皿があるからです」

Then he examined the chair carefully and noticed a dog leash tied to one corner of the bed. "Very unusual, is it not, Watson?"

"Yes, sir, very strange."

"I have seen enough now, Miss Stoner. Let us walk outside. It is very important that you follow my advice exactly, ma'am."

"Of course, I shall most certainly do so," she replied.

"Both my friend and I must spend the night in your room."

At this, both Miss Stoner and I looked at him in astonishment.

"You must stay in your old room; say that you have a headache when your stepfather returns home. Open the windows and put your lamp in the window, then go to your room even though it is being torn up by the builders. I think you can manage there for one night."

"Oh, yes, easily."

"The rest you will leave in our hands."

"But what will you do?"

"We shall spend the night in your room and investigate the cause of this noise which you have heard."

"I believe that you already know the cause."

"I believe I do."

"Please tell me."

"I will have proof before I speak, please."

■ dog leash 犬用の革ひも　■ in astonishment 驚いて　■ headache 图 頭痛　■ even though たとえ〜としても　■ torn 動 tear（〜を引き裂く）の過去分詞形　■ tear up ズタズタに引き裂く、引きはがす　■ builder 图 建築業者　■ manage 動 何とかやっていく　■ rest 图 後のこと　■ leave in someone's hands （人）に任せる　■ investigate 動 〜を捜査する　■ proof 图 証拠

それからホームズは椅子を注意深く調べ、ベッドの隅に犬用の革ひもが巻きつけてあるのに気づいた。「随分変わっているじゃないか、ワトソン君?」

「確かに。随分変わっている」

「十分拝見しましたよ、ストーナーさん。外を歩きましょう。私のアドバイスを確実に実行していただくことが重要なのですよ」

「もちろん、おっしゃる通りに致します」ストーナー嬢は答えた。

「ワトソンと私は今晩、あなたの寝室で過ごすことにします」

これには、ストーナー嬢も私も仰天してホームズを見た。

「あなたはご自分の元の寝室で過ごすのです。父上が戻ったら、頭痛がすると言って今の寝室にお引き取りなさい。窓を開けて、ランプを窓のくぼみに置いてから、元の寝室に入るのです。取り壊し中であると言っても、一晩なら大丈夫でしょう」

「簡単なことですわ」

「あとのことは我々に任せてください」

「でも、どうなさるおつもりですの?」

「我々は、あなたが現在使っている寝室で一晩を過ごし、あなたの聞いた物音の原因を究明します」

「もう原因がお分かりでいらっしゃいますのね」

「そう思います」

「教えてくださいませ」

「証拠を押さえてからということにさせてください」

"Well, am I right in thinking that she died of fright?"

"No, I do not think so. I think there was a real cause. Now, we must leave you, Miss Stoner. If your father saw us, our visit would be useless. Please excuse us. Be brave, for if you do as I have told you, you may be sure that the danger will soon be over."

Sherlock Holmes and I took a room at a nearby inn and from our window we saw Dr. Roylott pass by at dusk.

As we were waiting at the inn, Holmes turned to me and said, "You know Watson, I am afraid to take you with me. It is a dangerous evening I have planned."

"Can I help you?"

"Very much."

"Then I shall go with you. But I do not know what the danger is you saw."

"It is odd that the rope and hole in the ceiling are added to the room, and shortly afterward the woman who sleeps there dies. Didn't you notice anything odd about the bed?"

"No."

"It was fixed to the floor. Have you ever seen that before?"

"I cannot say that I have... Holmes! I see what you are saying."

"Well, the night will be frightening enough. Let us now think of something more cheerful."

■ die of（人が）〜が原因で死ぬ ■ fright 图 強い恐怖 ■ useless 厖 使い物にならない ■ over 厖 終わって ■ inn 图 宿屋 ■ pass by 通り掛かる ■ at dusk 夕暮れに ■ be afraid to 〜するのを怖がる ■ odd 厖 奇妙な ■ add 勔 付け足す ■ shortly afterward その後まもなく ■ fix 勔 〜を固定する ■ frightening 厖 恐ろしい ■ cheerful 厖 陽気な、愉快な

「では、姉は恐怖のあまり死んだのでございますね?」

「いいえ、そうは思いません。原因は別にあると考えています。さあ、失礼しますよ、ストーナーさん。父上が我々の姿を見たら、すべてが水の泡になってしまいます。ですから失礼させていただきます。私が言うとおり、気をしっかりともっていれば、危険はすぐに去っていきます」

シャーロック・ホームズと私は近くの宿に部屋を取った。夕暮れ時、そこの窓からドクター・ロイロットが帰宅するのが見えた。

宿で待機していると、ホームズが向き直っていった。「ねえワトソン、君を連れて行くのは気が引ける。今夜の計画は危険なのだ」

「私が役に立つのかね?」

「大いに」

「ならば、同行する。君の考える危険とはどういうものか見当もつかないがね」

「あの呼び鈴ロープと天井の穴が後から付けられて、その直後にあの部屋で寝た女性が死んだのはおかしい。ベッドを見たとき、変なことに気づかなかったか」

「いいや」

「床に固定してあったんだ。そういうのを見たことがあるかね?」

「無いなあ……　ホームズ!　君の言いたいことがわかったぞ」

「うむ、今夜は十分恐怖に満ちているのだから、今は楽しいことを考えるとしよう」

The house became dark about nine o'clock. Two hours passed slowly and then just at eleven, a single bright light appeared in the window.

"We must go," Holmes said.

A moment later we were on a dark road, with a cold wind in our faces. We had no difficulty entering the area of the house. Soon we had taken off our shoes and had climbed into the bedroom.

"We must sit in the dark. Do not go to sleep. Your very life depends on it," Holmes whispered to me. "I will sit on the bed and you sit in that chair."

I did as he said and laid my gun on the table. Holmes laid his cane on the bed.

I will never forget that night. I sat wide awake. I knew that Holmes was a few feet away, also wide awake. We waited in complete darkness. One, two and three o'clock came and went. Nothing happened. Suddenly a light was lit in the doctor's room. There was a smell of hot metal. Then another half hour passed. Suddenly, we heard a very soft sound, like steam from a kettle. At this Holmes sprang from the bed, lit the lamp and began waving his cane at the hole in the ceiling.

"Do you see it, Watson?" he cried out.

But I saw nothing—only that his face was white and frightened.

■ take off one's shoes 靴を脱ぐ　■ life 图 命、生命　■ depend on ～次第である
■ laid 動 lay（置く）の過去形　■ cane 图 杖、ステッキ　■ wide awake まんじりともせ
ずに　■ feet 图 フィート《長さの単位、約30.48cm》　■ steam 图 湯気　■ kettle 图 やか
ん　■ sprang 動 spring（跳ねる）の過去形

　館は午後9時頃、暗くなった。2時間がゆっくりと過ぎて、丁度11時に、窓のところに一点の明かりがともった。

　「行こう」ホームズが言った。

　すぐに我々は、冷たい風を頬に受けながら夜道を急いだ。敷地内に入るのは簡単だった。急いで靴を脱いで寝室に入り込んだ。

　「暗がりに座っていなければならないぞ。眠るなよ。命がかかっているのだからな」ホームズが囁いた。「私はベッドに座る。君はそこの椅子に座ってくれ」

　彼の言った通りにして、銃をテーブルの上に置いた。ホームズもステッキをベッドの上に置いた。

　あの夜のことは決して忘れないだろう。私はしっかり起きて座っていた。ホームズも、数フィート先で同じように起きているのがわかっていた。完全な暗闇の中で待つ。1時、2時、そして3時が来て、過ぎたが、何も起こらなかった。突然、ドクターの部屋に明かりがつき、金属を熱する匂いがした。さらに30分が過ぎた。突然、非常に柔らかな、やかんの蒸気のような物音が聞こえた。同時にホームズがベッドから飛び起きてランプをつけ、ステッキを天井の穴に向かって振り回し始めた。

　「見えるか、ワトソン?」ホームズが叫んだ。

　だが私には何も見えなかった――見えたのは、蒼白で恐怖に満ちたホームズの顔だけだ。

When he stopped, there was a terrible cry from the next room. We heard later that people in the village got out of their beds, it struck such coldness in the hearts of those who heard.

"What does that mean?" I asked.

"It means it's all over," Holmes replied.

"We are going into the doctor's room, now."

We found the safe door open with Dr. Roylott sitting dead in the chair. He was wearing a strange yellow band, with brownish speckles, around his head.

"The band, the speckled band!" whispered Holmes.

But it was not cloth. It was a yellow snake that had wound itself around the man's head.

"It is a swamp adder!" cried Holmes, "the deadliest snake in India. The doctor died within ten seconds of being bitten. Violence does come back to the violent. The schemer falls into the pit he digs for another. Let us put the snake back in his cage and take Miss Stoner to a safe place. Then we must tell the police what has happened."

These are the facts of the death of Dr. Roylott of Stoke Moran. We took the daughter to her aunt's, who gave her all the care she needed. Then the slow process of the official investigation began. The conclusion was that the doctor met his death while he was playing with a dangerous pet.

■ village 图 村　■ struck 動 strike（〜を引き起こす）の過去形　■ those who 〜する人々　■ all over すべて終わって　■ brownish 形 茶色がかった　■ cloth 图 布　■ wound 動 wind（〜を巻きつける）の過去分詞形　■ swamp adder 沼毒蛇　■ deadly 形 極めて有害な　■ bitten 動 bite（かむ）の過去分詞形　■ schemer 图 謀略家

ホームズがステッキを振り回すのを止めた時、隣室から恐ろしい叫び声が聞こえた。聞いた者の心を凍りつかせるような叫びで、村人たちがベッドから跳ね起きたと後で聞いた。

「どういうことなんだ?」私は尋ねた。

「すべてが終わったということさ」ホームズが答えた。

「ドクターの部屋へ行こう」

金庫のドアが開いて、ドクター・ロイロットが椅子に座ったまま死んでいるのが見つかった。頭には、褐色の斑点でまだらになった、奇妙な黄色の紐(バンド)が巻きついていた。

「紐だ、まだらの紐!」ホームズが囁いた。

だがそれは布ではなかった。黄色い蛇がドクターの頭に巻きついていたのだ。

「沼毒蛇だ!」ホームズが叫んだ。「インドで最強の猛毒蛇だ。ドクターは噛まれて10秒で絶命している。暴虐は、暴虐者に帰するということだ。他人を落とそうと掘った穴に自ら落ちたのだ。蛇を檻に戻したら、ストーナー嬢を安全なところに移そう。それから警察に事の次第を話すのだ」

以上がストーク・モランのドクター・ロイロットの死の顛末の真実である。我々はストーナー嬢を叔母のところに連れて行き、叔母がしっかりと面倒を見てくれた。その後、遅々とした警察の捜査が始まった。結果は、ドクターが危険なペットと戯れていて死んだということだった。

■ fall into the pit 穴に落ちる　■ cage 图 おり、ケージ　■ process 图 一連の行為　■ official 形 公式な　■ investigation 图 捜査　■ conclusion 图 結論　■ meet one's death 最期を遂げる

On the train back to London the next day, Holmes told me that he had gotten all the wrong ideas to begin with.

"Then I realized that the danger was not from the window or the door, but from the hole in the ceiling. The bed was fixed to the floor so that the rope could be used as a bridge for something to be passed through the wall and come down to the bed. The idea of a snake instantly occurred to me. Using a poison that is not commonly known to science was the idea that such a cruel man would have. Only a very sharp-eyed coroner would see too little holes made by a snake bite. The doctor trained the snake to return to his bedroom when it had completed its work.

"I had examined his chair. It was clear that he used to stand on it. I had no doubts when I saw the milk, the leash and the safe. The metallic noise Miss Stoner heard was the door of the safe closing as her father replaced the snake into its cage. Then I waited for the snake to come through the hole. When I heard its hiss, as I am sure you did, I lit the lamp and attacked it."

"So it turned back into the doctor's bedroom."

"And attacked him instead of us. In this way, I am responsible for the man's death, but I cannot say that I feel very sad about it or that it will weigh heavily on my conscience."

■ to begin with 最初は ■ instantly 副 すぐに ■ occur 動 頭に浮かぶ ■ commonly 副 一般に ■ sharp-eyed 形 目の利く ■ snake bite ヘビの咬みあと ■ replace 動 ～を元(の位置)に戻す ■ hiss 名 シューという音 ■ turn back 引き返す ■ responsible 形 責任がある ■ weigh 動 重荷になる ■ conscience 名 良心

翌日、ロンドンへ戻る列車の中でホームズが、自分は当初は全く間違った考えをしていたのだと語った。

「その後、危険は窓やドアからではなく、天井の穴から来たに違いないと気がついたのだ。ベッドが固定してあったのは、何かが壁からベッドに降りてくることができるよう、ロープを橋渡しに使うためだ。蛇のことが即座に頭に浮かんだ。一般の科学に知られていない毒を使うとは、あの残酷な男の思いつきそうなことだ。余程目の鋭い検死官でなければ蛇の咬み跡のような小さな穴は見逃してしまうだろう。奴は、仕事が終わったら自分の寝室に戻るよう、蛇を調教していたのだ。

ドクターの椅子を調べたら、上に立つのに使っていることが明らかだった。ミルクと革ひもと金庫を見た時には確信したね。ストーナー嬢の聞いた金属音は、蛇を檻に戻してから金庫の扉を閉める音だったのだ。それから、蛇が穴から降りてくるのを待った。シューっという音、君も聞いただろうが、あれが聞こえたとき、ランプを付けて蛇を攻撃したのだ」

「それで蛇はドクターの部屋に逃げ戻ったのだな」
「そして我々の代わりに、ドクターを襲ったのだ。その意味で、私は奴の死に責任があることになる。だが悲しいとか、良心が痛むとかいうことは全く言えないね」

覚えておきたい英語表現

> He always worked for the love of his art rather than for money. （p.92, 3行目）
> ホームズは常に、金のためではなく、己の手腕を発揮できる仕事を愛したのだ。

【解説】
for the love of 〜 は、「〜を大切に思う、重視するため」の意味です。ホームズの仕事ぶりはまさにart（芸術）です。従って、for the love of his work（仕事への愛）ではなく、for the love of his art（アートへの愛）と表現されています。人は、自分がもっとも大切にすることや人のために、行動し、生きます。あなたの人生で、アートと呼べることはなんでしょうか？

【例文】 ① I would do it for the love of our friendship.
　　　　僕たちの友情のために、引き受けよう。

　　　② Live for the love of your art rather than for fame.
　　　　名声よりも、愛する芸術のために生きよ。

> We will make everything all right. （p.96, 1行目）
> 我々がすべてを上手く収めましょう。

【解説】 不安げな相手を安心させる表現です。「心配しなくても、我々にまかせて。なんとかするので大丈夫」という意味の心強い表現ですから、覚えておきましょう。

【例文】 ① We will make sure of everything.
　　　　すべてをきちんと確認するよ。

　　　② Everything is going to be alright.
　　　　だいじょうぶ。
　　　　＊「心配しなくても、すべてうまくいくよ」という、励ましの表現です。

You are quite right. （p.96, 12行目）
おっしゃる通りでございます。

【解説】 quite（まったく）は、その後に続く単語を強調する副詞です。イギリス英語で頻繁に使用されます。quiteにアクセントを置いて発音します。

【例文】 ① I am quite sure.
私は確信を持っています。

② She is quite lovely.
彼女は非常に麗しい。

Your very life depends on it. （p.124, 8行目）
命がかかっているのだからね。

【解説】 Your very lifeのveryは、「まさに、ほかならぬ」という意味の形容詞として使われ、life（命）の尊さを強調しています。
depends on 〜 は、「〜に依存する、かかっている」の意味です。

【例文】 ① Your very life is at stake.
まさに君の人生がかかっている。

② Q : Do you prefer to stay at home on weekends?
A : It depends.
Q：週末は家にいる方がいいですか？
A：時と場合によります。

＊It depends.は、It depends on many things.（いろいろなことや状況によって異なります）の短縮形。はっきり答えられないときに使える便利な表現です。

THE
OF THE

空家の冒険

ADVENTURE
EMPTY
HOUSE

シャーロキアンにとっては最高傑作だが、
はじめてホームズ物語を読む人にはちょっと説明が必要だろう。
じつはホームズ物語を26作書いたところで、
ドイルは人気絶頂だったホームズを「殺してしまった」のだ。
『最後の事件』という作品のなかで、犯罪の帝王モリアーティ教授と
組み合ったままスイスの滝のなかに落ちたという設定であった。
ドイルは歴史文学を書くのが自分の本当の使命であると考えていたからだ。

もちろんホームズ・ファンからは大ブーイングが巻き起こった。
「私がほんとうに人を殺してもこんな非難は受けなかっただろう」と
ドイルは書いている。

この作品はそれから10年後に発表されたものである。
日本の「バリツ」という武術をやっていたおかげでホームズだけが助かり、
その後3年間世界を放浪したのち、ワトソンの前に姿をあらわす。
……その復活の見事な演出。
ファン達の歓声が聞こえるような作品である。

The Adventure of the Empty House

It was in the spring of the year 1894 that all London was interested in the murder of the Honorable Ronald Adair. Although the public learned much about the crime from the law case reported in the newspapers, a lot was not reported as the police did not need to bring forward all the facts. Only now, at the end of ten years, am I allowed to supply the missing pieces which make the story complete. The crime was of interest in itself, but more interesting was perhaps the most remarkable and surprising thing that ever happened to me. Even now, after all this time, I find my blood racing as I think of it. I would of course have loved to have shared my knowledge with those people who have shown interest in the thoughts and actions of a remarkable man. However, the great man himself would not allow me to speak of it until last month.

■murder 图 殺人 ■Honorable 图 閣下《敬称》 ■public 图 公衆 ■law case 訴訟事件 ■bring forward 公にする、公開する ■supply 動 供給する ■missing pieces 未解明の部分 ■remarkable 形 注目に値する ■race 動 駆け巡る

134

空家の冒険

　ロナルド・アデア卿殺人事件がロンドン中の人々の関心の的となったのは、1894年春のことであった。この殺人については新聞で報道された訴訟内容から、かなりのところは周知の事実となっているが、警察がすべてを公にする必要はなかったために、報道されていない内容も相当ある。それから10年がたとうとする今になって、私はようやく、この事件の全体像を明らかにするために必要な情報の断片を提供することを許可された。この事件はそれ自体、興味深いものである。しかし、それ以上に興味深いのは、おそらく、私の人生で起こった最も印象的で衝撃的な出来事であった。長い時間が経過した今ですら、あの時のことを思い出すと、背筋がぞくぞくするのがわかる。もちろん私は、ひとりの類まれなる人物の思考と行動に興味をおもちの方々に、私の得た情報をお伝えしたいと思ってきた。しかし、先月になるまで、その人物自身から公表を止められていたのだ。

My close friendship with Sherlock Holmes had interested me deeply in crime, and even after he went missing I still read about the various problems which came before the public. I even attempted, more than once, to use his methods to find the answer, though without great success. There was no case, however, which interested me as much as the sad story of Ronald Adair. The police knew that Mr. Adair had been murdered but were unable to discover who had done it. Their job was made more difficult because they could find no reason for the crime. There were points about this strange business which would, I was sure, have interested Sherlock Holmes. All day as I went upon my rounds, I thought about the case but could find no answer that seemed to be sensible.

The Honorable Ronald Adair was the second son of the Earl of Maynooth, at that time living in Australia. Adair's mother had returned from Australia to have an eye operation, and she, her son Ronald, and her daughter Hilda were living together at 427 Park Lane. The young man had many good friends in town and, so far as was known, had no enemies and had never upset anyone. Yet it was to this rich, easy-going young man that death came, in the most strange and unexpected way, between the hours of ten and eleven-twenty on the night of March 30, 1894.

■go missing 行方不明になる ■come before ～の前に現れる ■attempted 動 ～を試みる、企てる ■go upon ～に取り掛かる ■one's rounds 回診 ■sensible 形 理にかなっている ■Earl 名 伯爵 ■operation 名 手術 ■so far as was known 今までに知られている限り ■easy-going 形 のんきな、気楽な ■unexpected 形 思いも寄らない

　私はシャーロック・ホームズと親しくしていたことから、犯罪に強い興味を
もつようになった。彼がいなくなった後も、公にされるさまざまな事件を読み
ふけった。一度ならず、彼の手法を使って解決してみようと試みたことすらあ
るが、たいした成果はあげられなかった。それでも、ロナルド・アデアの悲劇
ほど興味をひかれた事件はなかった。警察は、アデア卿が殺されたことはわ
かっていたものの、犯人を見つけることができなかった。しかも、この犯罪に
は動機が見当たらず、それが解決をいっそう難しいものにしていた。私は、こ
の奇妙な事件にはホームズの関心をひくものがあるに違いないと確信してい
た。往診に出かけるかたわら、私はずっと事件について考えた。でも、納得で
きるような答えは見つからないでいた。

　ロナルド・アデア卿は、当時オーストラリアに住んでいたメイヌース伯爵の
次男にあたる。アデア卿の母親は、目の手術を受けるためにオーストラリアか
ら帰国していて、息子のロナルド、娘のヒルダと一緒にパークレーン427番地
に住んでいた。この青年には地域に良い友達がたくさんいて、知られている限
りでは敵はなく、誰かの敵意を買うこともないようであった。しかし、この裕
福でのんびりした青年が、1894年3月30日の午後10時から11時20分の間に、
非常に奇妙な予期せぬ死を迎えることとなった。

Ronald Adair liked playing cards, and played often, but never for an amount that would hurt him. He was a member of several card clubs. After dinner on the day of his death he had played cards at the Bagatelle club. The people who had played with him—Mr. Murray, Sir John Hardy, and Colonel Moran—had said that there was a fairly equal fall of cards. Adair might have lost five pounds, but not more. He had a lot of money and such a loss could not in any way affect him. He had played nearly every day at one club or another, but he was a careful player and usually ended up a winner. It came out in evidence that playing with Colonel Moran, he had actually won as much as four hundred pounds some weeks before from Godfrey Milner and Lord Balmoral.

On the evening of the crime, he returned from the club at ten. His mother and sister were out spending the evening with a friend. The servant reported that she heard him enter the front room on the second floor, generally used as his sitting room. She had made up a fire there and she had opened the window to let the smoke out. No sound was heard from the room until eleven-twenty when Lady Maynooth and her daughter returned. She wanted to say good-night to her son but found his room locked on the inside. He did not reply to their cries. They got help and the door was forced open. Ronald Adair was found lying near the table. It was clear from the state of the body that he had been shot by an expanding bullet, but no gun of any sort was to be found in the room.

■amount 图 量、金額　■fairly 圖 極めて、ほとんど　■equal 形 同等の　■fall of cards トランプの結果　■loss 图 損失額　■in any way 決して　■affect 動 ～に影響を及ぼす　■end up 最後は～に落ち着く　■come out 判明する　■Lord 图 卿《称号》

　ロナルド・アデアはカードゲームが好きで、よく遊んではいたが、身を滅ぼすような額を賭けることはなかった。いくつかのカードクラブのメンバーで、亡くなった日の夕食後は、バガテルというクラブで勝負をしていた。彼と一緒にいたマリー氏、ジョン・ハーディ卿、モラン大佐の証言によれば、勝負は引き分けだったとのことだ。アデアは負けたとしてもせいぜい5ポンド。裕福な彼にとって、それぐらいの散財は痛くもかゆくもない。彼はほとんど毎日、どこかのクラブでプレーしていたが、その賭けぶりは慎重だったので、通常は勝利をおさめた。証言によると、数週間前、モラン大佐とペアを組んで、ゴドフリー・ミルナーとバルモーラル卿に対して、400ポンドもの大金を獲得していたという。

　事件の夜、彼は10時にクラブから帰宅した。母と妹はその夜、友人と一緒にでかけていて留守だった。使用人は、彼がいつも居間として使っている三階正面の部屋に入る音を聞いたと証言している。彼女がそこで火を入れ、窓をあけて煙を外に出した。11時20分にメイヌース夫人と娘が帰宅するまで、部屋から物音は聞こえなかった。夫人は息子におやすみを言おうとしたところ、部屋は内側から鍵がかかっており、大声で呼んでも返事はなかった。助けを呼び、なんとか部屋を開けた。ロナルド・アデアはテーブル脇に横たわった姿で見つかった。その状態から、彼が拡張弾で撃たれたことが見てとれたが、部屋には銃らしきものは見あたらなかった。

■make up a fire 火に燃料を供給する　■get help 助けを得る［呼ぶ］　■state 名 状態
■expanding bullet 拡張弾

The Adventure of the Empty House

On the table was some money grouped in different amounts. There were also some figures upon a piece of paper, with the names of some club friends opposite them, from which it was judged that before his death he was trying to make out his losses or winnings at cards.

A further investigation only made the case harder to understand. In the first place, no reason could be given why the young man should have locked the door from the inside. There was the possibility that the murderer had done this, and had afterwards escaped from the window. The drop was at least twenty feet, however, and a bed of flowers lay beneath. Neither the flowers nor the earth showed any sign of someone having landed there, nor were there any marks on the grass which separated the house from the road. It appeared, therefore, that the young man himself had fastened the door. But how did he come by his death? No one could have climbed up to the window without leaving a mark. Suppose a man had fired through the window, it would indeed have been a remarkable shot to have caused so deadly a wound from such a distance. Also Park Lane is a busy road; there are people about at all hours but no one had heard a shot. But there was the dead man, and the soft-nosed bullet, which had expanded on hitting Adair, thereby making a wound which must have caused Adair's death at once. These facts of the Park Lane Mystery made even less sense when no reason could be found for the crime.

■figure 图 数字　■opposite 前 ～に向かい合って　■make out まとめ上げる　■winning 图 もうけ　■further 形 さらなる　■possibility 图 可能性　■murderer 图 殺人者　■drop 图 落差　■bed of flowers 花壇　■lay 動 lie（位置する）の過去形　■lie beneath ～の下にある　■neither A nor B AでもなくBでもない　■land 動 着地する

テーブルには、金がいくつかの山に積み上げられていた。数字と対戦したクラブの友人の名前が書かれた紙があり、彼が死ぬ前に、カードゲームでの勝ち負けを計算しようとしていたのだと思われた。

　さらに捜査をすすめたところ、事件はますます複雑になった。第一に、青年が内側から扉の鍵を掛けなければならない理由がわからない。犯人が鍵をかけ、その後、窓から逃走した可能性はある。しかし、高さは少なくとも20フィートあり、下には花壇がある。花にも地面にも踏まれた跡はなく、家と道との間にある草地の上にも足跡はなかった。したがって、青年自身が扉を閉めたのだと思われた。でも、彼はどのように死を迎えたのだろうか。足跡を残さずに窓まで登るのは無理だ。窓の外から発砲したとすると、これほどの距離から致命的な傷を負わせるのは至難の業である。また、パークレーンは賑やかな通りで、人通りが絶えることはなかったのに、銃の音を聞いたという者はいなかった。それでも、男の死体と、ソフトノーズの柔頭銃弾が残されていた。弾頭のやわらかい弾丸はアデアを撃った瞬間、きのこ状にひしゃげて、一瞬で致命傷を与えた。これがパークレーン事件の概要であるが、動機がみあたらないために解決の糸口がなかった。

■therefore 副 従って　■fasten a door　戸締まりをする　■come by（被害など）を受ける　■busy road　交通量が多い道路　■about 副 周囲に、動き回って　■soft-nosed bullet　柔かい弾頭の銃弾　■expand 動 拡大する、広がる　■thereby 副 その結果　■wound 名 外傷　■at once　即座に　■make even less sense　なおさら考えにくい

As I have said, young Adair was not known to have any enemies, and no attempt had been made to remove the money or valuables in the room.

All day I turned these facts over in my mind, trying to find an answer which would make sense of them, as well as the simple idea which Holmes had said was the starting point of every investigation. I must say that I was unsuccessful. In the evening I went for a walk and found myself about six o'clock at the Oxford Street end of Park Lane. There was a group of people all looking up at the same window; this was the house which I had come to see. A tall, thin man with colored glasses, whom I thought to be a plain-clothes detective, was pointing out his answer. The others crowded round to listen to what he said, but his thoughts seemed to me to be rather foolish. As I left the crowd I struck against a man almost doubled up with age and illness, causing him to drop several books which he was carrying. I remember that as I picked them up, I saw the title of one of them, a strange book about trees, and it struck me that the fellow must be some poor booklover, who, either as a trade or as a pastime hunted down unusual books. I tried to say I was sorry but it was clear that these books were very important objects to their owner. With an angry look he turned away, and he made his way through the crowd.

■attempt 图 試み、企て ■valuables 图 貴重品 ■turn ~ over in one's mind ～をよくよく考える ■make sense つじつまが合う ■go for a walk 散歩に出掛ける ■glasses 图 眼鏡 ■plain-clothes detective 私服刑事 ■point out ～を指摘する ■crowd round 取り囲む ■double up 二つ折りになる ■pastime 图 気晴らし、道楽 ■hunt down 見つけ出す ■object 图 物 ■make one's way through ～を通り抜ける

先に述べたとおり、アデア青年には敵がいた様子はなく、部屋から金や貴重品を持ち出そうとした形跡もなかった。

　私は一日中、これらの事実を振り返り、納得できるような解決や単純明快な発想——ホームズがかつて言っていた全ての調査の出発点となるもの——を見つけようとしたが、はっきりいって、うまくいかなかった。その夜、私は散歩していて、気が付くと6時ごろ、パークレーンのオックスフォード街側のはずれに来ていた。人々が群れをなし、皆がひとつの窓を見あげていた。これが私が見に来た家だ。色つき眼鏡をかけた背の高い、痩せた男性——私服刑事だろう——が持論を展開し、集まった人たちは彼の話を聴いていた。でも、彼の言うことは私にはばかばかしく思えた。その場から去ろうとしたときに、年のせいか病気のせいかで、ほとんど二つ折りのように背中が曲がった老人にぶつかり、彼が持っていた本が何冊か地面に落ちてしまった。落ちた本を拾っていると、その中の一冊のタイトルが目に入った。木についてのマニアックな本だった。それで私は、この男は、商売なのか趣味か、いずれにしても、大衆向けではない本を集める哀れな本好きなのだろうと思った。私は謝ろうと思ったが、落としてしまった本が彼にとってはこのうえなく大切な品だったようで、男は怒りに満ちた表情で向きを変え、人混みの中に消えていった。

My time spent watching No. 427 Park Lane did little to clear up the problem in which I was interested. The house was separated from the street by a low wall about five feet high. It was perfectly easy, therefore, for anyone to get into the garden. However, the window was a different matter. There was nothing which could help even the best climber to get to it. In fact I was less certain of the answer than ever as I walked back to Kensington. I had not been in my study five minutes when the servant entered to say that a person wanted to see me. Remarkably, it was none other than the strange old booklover, his face looking out from a ring of white hair. His books, twelve of them at least, were under his right arm.

"You're surprised to see me, sir," said he, in a strange, dry voice.

"Yes, I am rather," I replied.

"Well I felt I should say sorry for my manner earlier. There was no ill-feeling meant. I am indeed thankful that you helped to pick up my books."

"It was nothing, good sir," said I. "May I ask how you knew where to find me?"

"Well, sir, I am a neighbor of yours. My little bookshop is at the corner of Church Street, and I'm very pleased to meet you, I am sure. Maybe you like books yourself, sir. Here's *Birds of England* and *Catullus*, and *The Holy War*—a good buy every one of them. With five books you could just fill that space on the second row. It doesn't look quite right, sir."

■clear up the problem 問題を解明する　■low 形 低い　■in fact 実のところ
■study 名 書斎　■remarkably 副 珍しいことに　■none other than ほかならぬ～
■a ring of ～の輪　■manner 名 態度　■ill-feeling 名 敵意、悪意

　私はパークレーン427番地の現場を観察して過ごしたが、興味をもっていた問題の解決はほとんどすすまなかった。家と道路は5フィート程度の低い塀で隔てられていた。だから、誰かが庭に入るのはごく簡単だ。しかし、窓はそうはいかない。よじのぼれるようなものが何もないので、岩登りの名人であっても窓まで辿りつくのは不可能だ。私は前よりももっと混乱して、ケンジントンに戻ることにした。書斎に入って5分もたたないころ、使用人がやってきて、私に会いたいという人が来ていると告げた。なんと、あの奇妙な本収集家の老人だった。白髪で縁取られた顔がのぞいている。本——少なくとも12冊はあった——を右手にかかえていた。

　「私が伺ったことに、さぞかし驚かれたでしょう」と老人は、奇妙な乾いた声で言った。

　「そのとおりです」と私は答えた。

　「さきほどの私の態度についてお詫びをしなければと思いまして。悪気はなかったのです。本を拾っていただき、本当に感謝しております」

　「いえ、当然のことですよ」と私は言った。「どうしてここがわかったのですか?」

　「実は、この近所に住んでいるのです。チャーチ街の角で小さな書店をやっており、お会いできてうれしかったのです。本当に。きっとあなたも本がお好きでしょう。『イギリスの鳥』、『カトゥルス詩集』、『聖戦』をお持ちしました。どれも掘り出し物ですよ。この5冊があれば、2番目の棚の隙間がちょうど埋まるでしょう。このままではちょっと雑然として見えますよ」

■Catullus 図 カトゥルス《Gaius Valerius Catullus、ローマの抒情詩人。前84頃–前54頃》 ■The Holy War『聖戦』 ■second row 2列目

I moved my head to look at the bookcase behind me. When I turned again Sherlock Holmes was standing smiling at me across my study table. I rose to my feet, stared at him for a few seconds unable to speak. Then it appears that I must have passed out for the first and only time in my life. A gray cloud passed before my eyes, and when it had cleared I found my shirt undone. I had the aftertaste of a strong drink in my mouth. Holmes was bending over my chair.

"My dear Watson," said the well-remembered voice, "I am so sorry. I had no idea that you would be so overcome."

I held him by the arms.

"Holmes!" I cried. "Is it really you? Can it indeed be that you are alive? Is it possible that you succeeded in climbing out of that awful drop?"

"Wait a moment," said he. "Are you sure you are really fit to talk about these things? I have given you a grave upset by my unnecessarily unusual reappearance."

"I am all right, but indeed, Holmes, I can hardly believe my eyes. Good heavens!" Again I held him and felt his thin arm. "Well you are real enough. I'm overjoyed to see you. Sit down and tell me how you got out alive from that fearful mountain."

■bookcase 图 書棚　■rise to one's feet 立ち上がる　■pass out 意識を失う　■for the first and only time in one's life 生涯で最初で最後のこととして　■shirt 图 (ワイ) シャツ　■undone 形 解いた、ほどけた　■aftertaste 图 あと味　■strong drink 度の強い酒　■bend over かがむ　■well-remembered 形 よく見知った　■overcome 動 圧倒する

私は振り返って、後ろの本棚を見た。そして向き直った時、シャーロック・ホームズが書斎の机の向こうに立ち、私に笑いかけているではないか。私は立ち上がり、何も言えないまま数秒間彼を見つめた。そしてその後失神してしまったようだ。こんなことは私の人生で後にも先にもこれきりである。灰色の雲が目の前を通り過ぎ、気が付くと、私はシャツの襟もとを緩められていた。口には気付け薬の後味があった。ホームズが私の椅子にかがみこんでいた。

「おお、ワトソン君」と聞き覚えのある声が聞こえる。「すまなかった。君がここまで驚くとは思ってもみなかったんだ」
私は彼の腕をつかんだ。
「ホームズ!」声が大きくなる。「本当に君か？　君は本当に生きているのか？あの恐ろしい奈落の底から這い上がってくることができたのか？」

「ちょっと待ってくれ」と彼は言った。「君、こんな話をしても本当に大丈夫か。僕は不要に奇をてらった登場をして君をひどく動揺させてしまったね」

「私は大丈夫だ。でも、本当に自分の目が信じられないよ、ホームズ。本当なんだな」私は再び彼をつかみ、彼の細い腕の感触を確かめた。「そうだな、本物だな。ああ、君に会えて本当にうれしいよ。座って、あの恐ろしい断崖からどうやって生きて帰ってこれたのかを話してくれないか」

■hold someone by the arms（人）の腕をつかむ　■climb out of ～を降りる　■awful 形 恐ろしい　■drop 名 急斜面、落下　■fit 形 適切である　■grave 形 深刻な、重大な ■unnecessarily 副 不必要に　■reappearance 名 再登場　■overjoyed 形 大喜びの ■get out alive 生還する　■fearful 形 恐ろしい

He sat across from me, and lit a cigarette in his old, carefree manner. He was dressed in the old clothes of the book dealer, but the rest of that person lay among the white hair and old books upon the table. Holmes looked even thinner than of old, and although his eyes were bright, there was a dead-white shade to his face. This told me that his life of late had not been a healthy one.

"I am glad to be able to stand straight, Watson," said he. "It is hard for a tall man to appear so short for such a length of time. Now, my dear fellow, we have, if I may ask for your help, a hard and dangerous night's work in front of us. Perhaps it would be better if I told you the whole story when that work is finished."

"I cannot wait, Holmes. I should much rather know now."

"You'll come with me tonight?"

"When you like and where you like."

"This is, indeed, like the old days. We shall have time for a mouthful of dinner before we go. Well, then, about that fall from the mountain. I had no great difficulty getting out of it, for the very simple reason that I never fell!"

"You never fell?"

■sit across from ～の向かい側に腰をおろす　■carefree 形 気楽な　■dealer 名 販売業者　■of old 昔の　■dead-white 形 死人のように青白い　■shade 名 陰影　■of late 最近の　■stand straight 真っすぐに立つ　■length of time 時間の長さ　■mouthful 形 少量、一口

　私と向かいあって腰をおろしたホームズは、昔どおりの無頓着な仕草で煙草に火をつけた。古本屋の店主の古ぼけた服を着ていたが、その人物の残像は白髪のかつらと古本としてテーブルの上に置かれていた。ホームズは以前よりも老いたというよりいっそうほっそりとして見えた。目には輝きがあったが、顔には青白い影が差していて、このところの彼の生活が健康的なものではないことが伺えた。

　「背中を伸ばして立つことができて嬉しいよ、ワトソン君」と彼は言った。「背の高い男にとって、こんなに長い時間、身体を縮めているのは辛いものなんだ。ところで君、もし協力が頼めるならば、これから、難しくて危険な夜の仕事があるんだ。それが終わってから、全部を説明した方がいいだろう」

　「待てないよ、ホームズ。今聞かせてほしいんだ」
　「今夜僕と一緒に来るかい？」
　「君が望むなら、いつでも、どこへでも」
　「これですっかり、昔に戻ったようだ。出かける前に軽く夕食をとる時間はある。よし、それでは、あの断崖から落ちた件について話そうか。そこから脱出するのはたいして難しくはなかった。ごく単純な理由さ。そもそも落ちてなんかいなかったのだ」
　「落ちていなかったって？」

"No, Watson, I did not. My note at the time to you was completely true. I had little doubt that I had come to the end of my life when I saw the figure of the dangerous Professor Moriaty standing upon the thin passage-way which led to safety. I saw what he meant to do in his cold, gray eyes. I spoke with him, therefore, and he allowed me to write the short note which you afterwards received. I left it with my cigarette-box and my stick, and I walked along the pass with Moriaty close behind. When I reached the end I stood waiting. He pulled no gun, but he rushed at me and threw his long arms around me. He knew that his own game was up and wanted to take me down with him. We fell together close to the edge, and I faced death. With God's help I was able to shake off his hold; with a fearful shout he wildly tried to regain his feet, threw his arms out to try and catch me, but went over. With my face still over the edge, I saw him fall a long way. Then he struck a rock before falling into the water."

I listened to this remarkable explanation, which Holmes gave as he smoked his cigarette.

"But the tracks!" I cried. "I saw, with my own eyes, that two went along the mountain pass and none returned."

■passage-way 图 通路　■led 動 lead（導く）の過去分詞形　■lead to（道などが）～に通じる　■mean to ～するつもりである　■cigarette-box 图 煙草入れ　■close behind すぐ後ろに　■rush at 襲い掛かる　■game is up すべて終わった　■take someone down（人）の高慢の鼻をへし折る　■shake off 振り払う　■regain his feet（転んだ状態から）起き上がる　■track 图 足跡　■mountain pass 山道、峠

「そうさ、ワトソン君、落ちなかったんだ。あの時僕が君に書いた手紙は全くもって本当さ。細い小道——そこを行けば逃げられたんだ——にあの危険なモリアーティ教授の姿を見た時、いよいよ僕の人生も終わりに来たと覚悟した。彼の冷たい灰色の瞳を見れば、彼の考えていることがわかった。だから僕は彼と話をして、後に君が受け取ることになる短い手紙を書くことを許してもらったのだ。僕はその手紙を煙草入れとステッキと一緒に置き、道を進んだ。モリアーティはすぐ後についてきていた。行き止まりまで来たので、僕はそのまま待った。彼は銃も出さずに僕につかみかかってきて、長い両腕を巻きつけた。彼は自分はこれで終わりだとわかっていて、僕を道連れにしたがっていたのだ。僕らはふたりして崖っぷちでよろめいた。死は目の前にあった。しかし、運よく僕は彼の手を振り払うことができた。彼は恐ろしい叫び声をあげて、なんとかして踏ん張りつづけようとし、腕を伸ばして私をつかもうとしたが、落ちていった。僕は顔を崖からつき出して、彼がはるか下へと落ちていくのを見た。彼は岩にぶつかり、それから水にのまれていったよ」

　ホームズが煙草をふかしながら続けるこの驚くべき説明に、私は聴き入った。

　「でも、足跡は!」と私は言った。「私はこの目で見たんだよ。2つの足跡が崖へと進んでいって、どちらも引き返した形跡はなかった」

"It came about in this way. The moment that the Professor had disappeared, it struck me what a really extraordinarily good chance Heaven had placed before me. I knew that Moriaty was not the only man who wanted to kill me. There were at least three others who would now be even angrier because of the death of their leader. They were all most dangerous men. One or other would surely get me. On the other hand, if all the world thought that I was dead, they would take chances, these men; they would lay themselves open. Sooner or later I could destroy them. Then it would be time for me to let everyone know that I was still in the land of the living. So quick does the mind act that I believe I had thought this all out before Professor Moriaty had reached the bottom of Reichenbach Fall.

"I stood up and looked at the rocky wall behind me. In your rather pretty account of the matter, which I read with great interest some months later, you said that the wall could not be climbed. That was not quite true. A few small footholds presented themselves, and I thought I could see a resting point higher up. The mountain wall was so high that to climb it all was not a possibility, and I could not have made my way along the wet path without leaving some tracks. I thought, then, it was best that I should chance the climb. It was not a pleasant business, Watson.

■come about 生じる　■extraordinarily 副 異例に　■place 動 ～を置く　■surely 副 疑いなく、確かに　■on the other hand 他方では　■sooner or later 遅かれ早かれ　■land of the living この世　■So quick does the mind act that 非常な速さで頭が働いた《程度を表す倒置「So + 形容詞」》　■fall 名 滝　■rocky wall 岩壁

「それはこういうわけだ。教授が消えた瞬間、僕は、これは天が与えたもう
た途方もなく素晴らしいチャンスなのだということに気付いた。僕を殺したい
と思っているのがモリアーティだけではないことはわかっている。少なくとも
あと3人いて、首領が死んだ今となってはますます逆上していることだろう。
この上なく危険な連中だ。このうち誰かが、きっと僕を殺すことになる。でも、僕が死んだと世間が思い込めば、奴らは油断して、正体を表すだろう。そ
して遅かれ早かれ、僕は奴らを始末することができる。その時こそ、僕がまだ
この地上に生きていることを皆に知らせる時だ。僕の頭は非常な速さで働いた
ので、モリアーティ教授がライヘンバッハの滝壺に届く前に、ここまで全てを
考え終えていたはずだよ。

　僕は立ち上がって、後ろの岩壁を見た。君、この事件についてなかなかの
記述をしていたね。何ヵ月かしてから、非常に面白く読ませてもらったよ。
君はその中で、壁は登ることができるようなものではなかったと言っていた
ね。それは事実とは違うんだ。小さな足場がいくつかあり、上の方には岩棚
もありそうだった。岩壁は高くて、最後まで登るのは無理だった。また、濡
れた小道を足跡を残さずに行くのも不可能だった。それで僕は、危険を覚悟
で登るのが最善だと思ったんだ。ワトソン君、楽しい仕事ではなかったよ。

■pretty 形 かなりの　■account 名 報告、記事　■foothold 名 足掛かり　■present
oneself 現れる　■resting point 休息場所　■make one's way along a path 小道に
沿って進む　■pleasant 形 楽しい　■business 名 (取り組むべき)仕事

The fall was beneath me, and although I am not easily fooled, I give you my word that I seemed to hear Moriaty's voice shouting at me from below. One misplaced foot would have meant my death, for real this time. More than once I thought I was gone. But I kept going upward. At last I reached a point several feet deep and covered with soft green grass, where I could lie unseen. There I lay when you, my dear Watson, and all your following were investigating, in your usual questionable way, the manner of my death.

"At last, when you had come to completely the wrong answer, you left for the hotel and I was alone. I had thought that I had reached the end of my problems, but there were still surprises in store for me. A great rock, falling from above, rushed past me, hit the track, and carried on into the fall. For a moment I thought that it was by chance, but, looking up, I saw a man's head against the darkening sky. Then another rock struck near the place where I was laying. Moriaty had not been alone. One of his men, and it was one of the most dangerous of Moriaty's group, had kept guard while the Professor and I had fought. From a distance, unseen by me, he had watched Professor Moriaty's death and my escape. He had waited, and then making his way round to the top of the mountain, he had tried to succeed where Moriaty had failed.

■fool 動 惑わす ■I give you my word 誓って言うが〜 ■misplaced 形 見当違いの ■for real 本当に ■upward 副 上へ ■unseen 形 目に見えない ■questionable 形 疑問の余地がある ■manner 図 やり方、方法 ■surprise in store for（人）を待ち受けている驚き ■carry on 続ける ■by chance 偶然に ■darkening 形 だんだん暗くなる ■from a distance 遠くから

滝が僕の足元で流れているんだ。僕は無意味な妄想をするような人間ではないが、モリアーティが滝壺の底から僕に向かって叫ぶ声が聞こえたような気がした。一歩でも足を踏み外したら、今度は本当に死ぬことになる。何度ももうだめだと思いながらも、上に進んだ。そしてとうとう、何フィートかの奥行があり、柔らかい緑の草で覆われている場所にたどり着いた。ここで横になって、姿を隠すことができたんだ。ワトソン君、君と君の仲間たち全員が、僕の死んだ状況を、君のいつもどおりの問題の多いやり方で調べていた時、僕はそこに寝転んでいたのさ。

　ついに君たちは全くもって間違った結論に達し、ホテルに向かって去っていって、僕はひとりになった。僕はこの問題はこれで終わりだと思っていたが、まだ驚くことが残っていた。巨大な岩が頭上から落ちてきて、僕の傍をかすめ、猛烈な勢いで転がり、道にぶつかって滝壺へと落ちた。一瞬、僕は事故だと思った。しかし、見上げると、暮れなずむ空を背に男の頭が見えた。その後、別の岩が僕が寝ていた岩棚のすぐそばにぶつかった。モリアーティはひとりではなかったのだ。彼の仲間、それも最も凶暴な人間が、教授と僕が取っ組み合いをしている間、見張りをしていた。彼は、離れた所から、僕に気付かれずに、モリアーティ教授が死んで僕が逃げるのを見ていた。彼は頃合いを見て崖の上に上り、モリアーティができなかったことをやりとげようとしたのだ。

The Adventure of the Empty House

"I did not take long to think about it, Watson. Again I saw that angry face look over the edge, and I knew that another rock was coming. I raced back down toward the path. I don't think I could have done it in cold blood. It was a hundred times more difficult than getting up. But I had no time to think of the danger, for another stone rushed past me. Halfway down I fell, but, thanks to God, I landed torn and bloody upon the path. I raced away, did ten miles over the mountains in the darkness, and a week later I found myself in Florence, knowing that no one in the world knew what had become of me.

"I told only one person—my brother Mycroft. I must say sorry to you, my dear Watson, but it was all important that I should be thought dead. I am sure that you would not have written so believable report of my unhappy end had you yourself not thought it were true. Several times during the last three years I have taken my pen to write to you, but always I feared that your kind feelings for me should lead you to say something which would give away my secret. For that reason I turned away from you this evening when you upset my books, for I was in danger at the time, and any show of surprise on your part might have led to the most unpleasant results. As to Mycroft, I had to tell him in order to get the money I needed. Things did not go as well in London as I had hoped, for the trial of the Moriaty group left two of its most dangerous members, my own most fearful enemies, still free.

■look over the edge 崖っぷちから下をのぞく　■race back 急いで引き返す　■in cold blood 冷静に　■rush past ～を急いで通り過ぎていく　■halfway 副 途中で ■bloody 形 血だらけの　■become of ～はどうなるのか　■would not have ～ had

156

　それについてそんなに長く考えることはなかったよ、ワトソン君。怒りに満ちた顔が崖を覗きこむのを再び目にして、僕は次の岩が落ちて来るのだとわかった。僕は小道に向かって這い降りた。自分が冷静にやり遂げたなんて思ってはいないよ。登るよりも百倍は難しかった。でも、危険を考えている暇はなかった。三つめの岩が傍をかすめ、僕は途中まですべり落ちた。でも神のご加護で、傷だらけ、血だらけになりながらも道に着地した。僕は走って逃げた。暗闇の中、山を越え10マイル走り、一週間後にフローレンスに着いていた。世界中の誰も、僕に何が起こったのかを知らないはずだという確信があった。

　僕はひとりだけに打ち明けた——兄のマイクロフトだ。君には本当に申し訳ないと思っているよ、ワトソン君。でも、僕が死んだと思われていることが非常に重要だったのだ。そして君自身がそれを真実だと思わなかったら、僕の不幸な最期についてあれほど説得力のある記述ができなかっただろうということもわかっている。この3年間、僕は何度も、君に手紙を書こうとペンを取った。でも、そのたびに、君が、僕に対するやさしい心遣いから、僕の秘密を暴くようなことを口にしてしまうのではないかという心配にかられた。そういったわけで、今晩君が僕の本をひっくり返した時、君に背中を向けたのだ。あの時、僕は危険の中にいた。君のどこかに驚きが少しでも見えてしまったら、悲惨な結末になっていたかもしれない。マイクロフトについては、僕が必要な金を送ってもらうために話をしておく必要があった。ロンドンでは、望んでいたようにはことはうまく進まなかった。というのは、モリアーティ一味の裁判で、最も危険な仲間のうち2人、僕が最も恐れている敵が放免されたのだ。

you yourself...《仮定法過去完了のifの省略で主語とhadが倒置》(if you yourself had → had you yourself) ■give away（秘密の情報を）漏らす ■unpleasant 形 不愉快な ■as to ～に関しては ■trial 名 裁判

157

I traveled for two years in distant countries. You may have read of
the remarkable travels of a Norwegian named Sigerson, but I am
sure that you did not know you were receiving news of your friend.
I kept myself busy doing various jobs, some for my own pleasure
and some of which I cannot speak. Then recently I learned that
only one of my enemies was now left in London, I was about to
return when my movements were quickened by the news of this
very remarkable Park Lane Mystery, which not only interested me
on its own, but which seemed to offer me a way in which I could
also help myself. I came over at once to London, called as myself
at Baker Street, threw Mrs. Hudson into a near fit, and found that
Mycroft had kept my rooms and my papers just as they had always
been. So it was, my dear Watson, that at two o'clock today I found
myself in my old room, and only wishing that I could have seen
my old friend Watson in the other chair."

Such was the remarkable story to which I listened on that
April evening—a story which would have been unbelievable
to me had it not been told by Holmes himself, my oldest friend,
whom I had never thought I would see again. In some way he had
learned of my own sad loss, and his feelings were shown in his
manner rather than his words. "Work is the best way to deal with
sorrow, my dear Watson," said he; "and I have a piece of work
for us both tonight which, if we can bring it to a successful end,
will be reason enough, by itself, for a man to live on this earth."

■Norwegian 図 ノルウェー人 ■offer 動 提供する ■come over to 〜にやって [移っ
て] 来る ■throw someone into （人）に〜を起こさせる ■fit 図 発作、引きつけ
■Such is 〜 これが〜である ■unbelievable 形 信じられない ■in some way 何らか
の方法で

158

僕は2年間、異国の地を旅行した。君はシガーソンというノルウェー人の面白い旅行記を読んだことがあるかもしれないが、僕は君が、友人から近況報告を受け取っているとは気づいていないと確信しているよ。僕はさまざまな仕事をして忙しく過ごした。楽しかったものもあれば、言いたくないものもあるよ。そして最近、残っている唯一の敵がロンドンにいると知って、僕はロンドンに戻ろうとしていた。そんな時、この非常に注目すべきパークレーン事件のことを聞いて、背中を押されたように感じた。事件自体に興味をひかれただけでなく、この事件が、僕個人の問題を解決する機会を提供してくれているように見えたんだ。それですぐにロンドンに来て、ベーカー街を変装せずに訪ね、ハドソン夫人にとんでもないショックを与えてから、マイクロフトが僕の部屋と書類を、かつてのままにしておいてくれたことを発見した。ワトソン君、それが今日の2時だ。僕はかつて住んでいた部屋で、こちらの椅子に旧友ワトソン君が座っていてくれたらなぁと願っていた」

　これがあの4月の夜、私が聞いた驚くべき話だ。二度と会うことはできないと思っていた旧友ホームズ自身によって語られたものでなかったら、とても信じることはできなかったと思う。彼は、どこからか私の身に起こった悲しい離別を知っていて、彼の思いやりは言葉ではなく態度で示された。「仕事は悲しみを癒す最高の薬だよ、ワトソン君」と彼は言った。「そして今夜、僕らの前にはちょっとした仕事がある。それをうまく解決できれば、それだけで、ひとりの男がこの地球に生きていることを正当化する理由になるよ」

I asked him to tell me more. "You will hear and see enough before morning," he answered. "We have three years of the past to talk about first. And at half past nine, we will start upon the adventure of the empty house."

It was indeed like old times when, at that hour, I found myself seated beside him in a cab, my gun in my pocket, and adventure in my heart. Holmes was quiet and deep in thought. I did not know what we were about to do, but I knew from Holmes's manner that the adventure was a dangerous one.

I had thought that we were going to Baker Street, but Holmes stopped the cab at the corner of Cavendish Square. I noticed that as he stepped out he gave a careful look to left and right, and at every street corner he took the same pains to see that we were not followed. We then took back street after back street as Holmes once again showed his remarkable knowledge of London. In the end we were in a small road, lined with old, dark houses, which led us into Manchester Street, and so to Blandford Street. Here he turned quickly down a small passage, passed through a wooden gate into an empty yard, and then opened the back door of a house with a key. We entered together, and he closed it behind us.

■half past ～時30分すぎ　■deep in thought 思案にふけって　■square 图 (四角い) 広場　■step out 外へ出る　■take pains to ～するように心を砕く　■back street 裏通り　■in the end 結局、ついに　■passage 图 (通りにくい場所の) 通路　■yard 图 中庭　■back door 裏口、勝手口

私は彼に、もっと話をしてほしいと頼んだ。「朝までには十分に見聞きできるよ」と彼は言った。「僕たちには話すことが過去3年分ある。9時半になったら、空家の冒険に出かけよう」

　その時刻、昔と全く同じように、私は馬車で彼の隣に座っていた。ポケットには拳銃をしのばせ、心は冒険にわくわくしていた。ホームズは静かに考え込んでいた。これから何がおこるのかわからなかったが、ホームズの態度から、この冒険が危険なものであることは察することができた。

　私はベーカー街に向かうのだろうと思っていたが、ホームズは馬車をキャベンディッシュ・スクエアの角で止めた。彼が外に出る時、左右を注意深く確認し、通りの角では毎回、つけられていないかを確認するのに心を砕いた。ホームズは再びロンドンに対する卓越した知識を発揮し、私たちは裏道から裏道へと歩いた。そして、古く陰気な家がたち並ぶマンチェスター街とブランフォード街に通じる小さな道に出た。ここで彼は狭い路地へ素早く飛びこんだ。木戸をくぐり抜け、さびれた庭に出た。そして鍵で家の裏戸を開けた。私たちは一緒に中に入り、彼が後ろで扉を閉めた。

The place was completely dark, but it was clear to me that it was an empty house. Holmes's cold, thin fingers closed round my arm and led me forward down a long hall, until I saw the street light over the front door. Here Holmes turned suddenly to the right, and we found ourselves in a large, square, empty room, very dark in the corners, but with just a little light in the center from the street outside. Even so we could only just see each other from a few feet away and the rest of the room was completely black. My friend put his mouth to my ear.

"Do you know where we are?" he said as quietly as possible.

"Surely that is Baker Street," I answered looking through the window.

"Just so. We are in Camden House, which stands across from our old quarters."

"But why are we here?"

"Because it gives such a good view of our old home. Might I trouble you, my dear Watson, to go a little closer to the window, taking every care not to show yourself, and then to look at our old rooms? We will see if my three years away have completely taken away my power to surprise you."

■close round ～を取り囲む ■square 形 四角い ■just so まさにその通りで
■across from ～の真向かいに ■quarter 名 地区、街区 ■take care not to ～しないように気を付ける ■see if ～かどうかを確かめる ■take away 取り上げる

　そこは真っ暗だったが、空家だということはわかった。ホームズの冷たく骨ばった指が私の腕をつかみ、私は長い廊下の奥にひっぱられていった。やがて玄関の扉の上に通りのうす明りが見えた。そこでホームズは突然右に曲がり、私たちは大きくて四角い部屋に来た。部屋の中には何もなく、隅は暗かった。部屋の中央には外の通りからかすかな光が入っていたが、それでも、数フィート先にあるお互いの姿をなんとか認識できる程度で、それ以外は真っ暗だった。友は私の耳元に口を近づけた。

　「どこにいるかわかるか」と彼は早口で言った。
　「あれは間違いなくベーカー街だ」と私は窓から外を眺めながら答えた。

　「その通り。僕らの懐かしい下宿屋の向かいに立つカムデン・ハウスの中にいるんだ」
　「でも、なぜここへ?」
　「ここからなら、僕らの下宿がよく見えるからさ。すまないが、ワトソン君、ちょっと窓に近づいてくれ。姿が見られないように十分に注意してくれたまえ。それから僕らの古い下宿を見てみてくれ。この3年間の年月が、君を驚かす力を僕から完全に奪ったかどうか確認してみよう」

I inched forward and looked across at the window. As my eyes fell upon it, I gave a cry of surprise. There was a strong light burning in the room and the outline of a man, seated in a chair, was clear to see. It could only be one person; it was a perfect reproduction of Holmes. So surprised was I that I threw out my hand to make sure that the man himself was standing beside me. He was shaking as he tried to stop himself laughing out loud.

"Well?" said he.

"Good heavens!" I cried. "It is remarkable."

"I trust you are suitably pleased," said he, and I heard in his voice the same joy a painter feels in his art. "It really is rather like me, is it not?"

"I can hardly believe it is not you."

"Monsieur Oscar Meunier, of Grenoble, made the likeness, and I set it up myself during my visit to Baker Street this afternoon."

"But why?"

"Because, my dear Watson, I have a reason for wishing some people to think that I was there when I was really elsewhere."

"And you thought the rooms were watched?"

"I knew they were."

"By whom?"

■inch 動 少しずつ動く　■look across at ～を遠巻きに見る　■fall upon ～に向かって行く　■outline 名 輪郭　■reproduction 名 複製品、コピー　■throw out （手などを）突き出す　■make sure that ～であることを確認する　■stand beside （人）の隣に立つ

　私は少しずつ前に進んで、窓から外を見た。そこを見たとき、驚きで大きな声を出してしまった。部屋の中にはこうこうと明かりがついていて、椅子に座っている男の影がはっきりと見えた。この輪郭は、あの人物以外にありえない。ホームズの完全な複製だった。あまりに驚いて、手を伸ばして実物が隣に立っているのを確かめたほどだ。彼は笑い出すのを我慢しようとして体を震わせていた。

「どう」と彼は言った。
「何なんだ!　信じられない」と私は叫んだ。
「喜んでくれたようだね」と彼は言った。その声には、画家が自分の作品に対して感じるのと同じ喜びが感じられた。「本当に僕に似ていると思わないかい?」
「君にしか見えないよ」
「グルノーブルのオスカル・ムニエ氏の作なんだ。今日の午後、ベイカー街を訪れた時に僕が準備しておいた」
「でも、何のために?」
「ワトソン君、僕が実際には別の場所にいるときに、僕があそこにいると思わせておきたい奴がいるからだ」
「あの部屋が見張られていると思ったのか?」
「間違いなく見張られている」
「誰に?」

■shake 動 震える　■laugh out loud 大笑いする　■suitably 副 ぴったり合って
■pleased 形 喜んで、気に入って　■joy 名 喜び　■likeness 名 似顔絵、肖像　■set
up 据え付ける　■elsewhere 副 他の場所に

"By my old enemies, Watson. By Moriaty's group. You must remember that they, and only they, knew that I was still alive. Sooner or later they believed that I should come back to my rooms. They watched them continuously, and this morning they saw me arrive."

"How do you know?"

"Because I knew their guard. I saw him when I looked out of my window. He is a harmless enough fellow, Parker by name. I cared nothing for him. But I cared a great deal for the person who was behind him, the best friend of Moriaty, the man who dropped the rocks from the mountain top, the most dangerous criminal in London. That is the man who is after me tonight, Watson, and that is the man who has no idea that we are after him."

My friend's plans were slowly becoming clear. From our position, the watchers were being watched and the trackers, tracked. That outline of the thin face across the road would bring our enemy, and we awaited them. In the quiet darkness we stood together and watched the hurrying figures who passed and repassed in front of us. Holmes did not move; but I could tell that he missed nothing, and that his eyes studied each and every passerby. It was a cold night, and the wind blew down the long street. There were many people about, most of them covered up in coats. Once or twice it seemed to me that I had seen the same figure before, and I noticed with interest two men who appeared

---

■continuously 副 継続的に　■guard 图 番人　■look out of（窓など）から外を見る ■harmless 厖 無害の　■by name 名前は（～という）　■great deal 大いに　■mountain top 山頂　■after 前 ～の後を追って　■watcher 图 監視人　■tracker 图 追跡者

「僕の古い敵にだよ、ワトソン君。モリアーティの一味さ。憶えているだろう、僕がまだ生きているということを、奴らが——奴らだけが知っているんだ。遅かれ早かれ、奴らは僕がこの部屋に戻ってくるはずだと踏んでいた。ずっと見張っていて、今朝僕が戻ってきたのを見つけた」

「どうしてわかった?」
「見張りの男に見覚えがあった。僕が窓から外を見た時に、顔を見たんだ。それほど害がない男さ。パーカーという名前だが、奴のことは気にしていない。しかし、やつの後ろにいる非常に恐ろしい人物は要注意だ。モリアーティの親友であり、崖の上から岩を投げ落とした男、ロンドンで最も危険な犯罪者だ。この男が、今夜僕を狙っている。そしてね、ワトソン君、この男は、僕らが彼を狙っていることに気付いていないのさ」

　ホームズの計画が少しずつわかってきた。この場所から、見張り役が見張られ、追跡者が追跡される。あの痩せた横顔が道路に映れば、敵をおびき寄せることができる。私たちは待った。無言で暗闇の中に並んで立ち、人々が急ぎ足で行きかうのを眺めた。ホームズは身動きをしなかったが、何ひとつ見落とすまいと、通り過ぎる一人一人をしっかりと見ていることがわかった。冷え込む夜で、風が長い通りを吹きぬけていた。大勢の人が行きかっていたが、ほとんどの人がコートを着込んでいた。一度か二度、以前に見かけた人物を見たような気がした。そして、通りを少し行った家の戸口で、風をよけるようにしている2人の男に注目した。私はそのことをホームズに話そうとしたが、彼は即座

to be keeping out of the wind in the doorway of a house some distance up the street. I tried to tell Holmes about them but he shook his head quickly and continued to stare into the street. It was clear to me that he was becoming uneasy and that his plans were not working out altogether as he had hoped. At last as it neared twelve o'clock and the street slowly cleared, he walked up and down the room unable to control his nerves. I was about to say something to him, when I raised my eyes to the lighted window, and felt almost as great a surprise as before. I pointed at it.

"The outline has moved," I cried.

It was indeed no longer the side, but the back, which was now turned towards us.

Three years had not made Holmes feel more kindly to minds less clever than his own.

"Of course it has moved," said he. "Am I such a fool, Watson, that I should place such a clear copy, and expect that some of the men of Moriaty's group would be fooled by it? We have been in this room two hours and Mrs. Hudson has made some change in that figure eight times, or once in every quarter of an hour. She works it from the front so that her outline may never be seen. Ah!"

■keep out of ～を避ける ■uneasy 形 不安な、焦って ■work out 成功する ■altogether 副 全く、全然 ■nerves 名 イライラすること ■lighted 形 火の灯っている ■no longer もはや～でない ■kindly 副 優しく ■once in every ～ごとに一度の割合で ■quarter of an hour 15分

に頭を振って、道を見続けた。ホームズの心が落ち着かず、計画が全体として思うようにいっていないというのは明らかだった。いよいよ12時近くになって、人通りが次第にまばらになってくると、彼は動揺を抑えきれず、部屋を行ったり来たりした。私が何か話しかけようとした時、ふと灯りのついた窓に目が留まった。そして、前回とほとんど変わらない大きな驚きに襲われた。私は指を指して叫んだ。

「影が動いた」

実際、影はこの時、横顔ではなく後ろ向き、つまりこちらに背を向けた姿になっていた。

3年の年月が流れても、ホームズの、自分よりも知性の劣る人間に対する辛辣さは変わっていなかった。

「もちろん動いたよ」と彼は言った。「ワトソン君。僕がそんなあからさまに人形だとわかるようなものを置いて、モリアーティの一味の誰かがそれに騙されると期待しているような間抜けに見えるかい？　僕らはもう2時間、この部屋にいる。ハドソン夫人はその間に、あの像を8回、つまり15分ごとに動かしているよ。自分の影が映らないように、前方からやってもらっているんだ。あ！」

He breathed deeply. In the low light I saw his head thrown forward, his whole body completely still as he looked. Outside the street was completely empty. Those two men might still be in the doorway, but I could no longer see them. All was still and dark, save only that lighted window in front of us with the black figure outlined upon its center. Again in the quiet I heard that thin note from Holmes which told me something was about to happen. A moment later he pulled me back into the darkest corner of the room, and I knew I must, at all costs, stay completely quiet. Never had I known my friend more moved, and yet the dark street was still empty before us.

But suddenly I noticed that which his senses had already picked up. A low sound came to my ears, not from the direction of Baker Street, but from the back of the very house in which we lay in wait. A door opened and closed. A moment later steps could be heard in the hall. Holmes moved back against the wall, and I did the same, my hand closing upon my gun as I moved. Looking into the darkness of the hall I could just make out the outline of a man, a shade blacker than the blackness of the open door. He stood for a moment and then came into the room. He was within three yards of us, this dangerous looking figure, and I had readied myself to meet his spring before I realized that he had no idea that we were there.

■thrown forward 前に投げられる　■doorway 图 戸口　■note 图 音、調子、雰囲気　■at all costs いかなる代償を払っても　■never had I known《倒置、否定語を文頭に置いて強調（否定語+V+S）》　■pick up ～に気が付く　■direction 图 方向、向き　■make out 認識する　■yard 图 ヤード《長さの単位、約91.44cm》　■ready oneself 用意する　■spring 图 飛び出すこと

彼ははっとして息をのんだ。薄暗い光の中で、彼が頭を突き出し、全身を硬直させて様子をうかがっているのがわかった。外の通りは人っ子ひとりいなかった。例の2人の男はまだ戸口にいるようだが、もうその姿を見ることはできなかった。全てが静かで暗く、目の前にある灯りのついた窓と、その中央に浮かんだ黒い人影が見えるだけであった。その静けさの中で、ホームズの細い息の音が聞こえた——何かが起ころうとしている。次の瞬間、彼は私を部屋の一番暗い隅に引っ張っていった。何があっても静かにしていなくてはならないのだとわかった。友がこれほど動揺したのを私は見たことがない。しかし、私たちの前の暗い通りには、あいかわらず誰もいなかった。

しかし突然、私は彼の感覚がすでに感知していた音に気付いた。低い音が、ベーカー街の方向からではなく、私たちが隠れているこの家の後ろから聞こえてきたのだ。扉が開き、閉じられた。次の瞬間、廊下を進む足音が聞こえた。ホームズは後ずさりして壁に背中を付け、私も、銃に手をかけながら同様の姿勢をとった。暗い廊下をのぞくと、開いた扉の暗闇よりもさらに黒い男の輪郭が確認できた。彼は一瞬立ち止まり、それから部屋に入ってきた。私たちから3ヤードと離れていないところにいる。この危険な人物がとびかかってくるのではと身構えたが、間もなく、彼が私たちの存在に気付いていないことがわかった。

He passed close beside us, over to the window, and noiselessly raised it half a foot. As he dropped to the height of this opening, the light of the street fell full upon his face. In his hand he carried what appeared to be a stick. Then from his coat he pulled a heavy object, and he placed the two pieces together. He straightened and I saw that what he held in his hand was a sort of gun. He opened it, put something in and closed it. Then, bending down, he rested the end of the gun upon the edge of the open window, and I saw his eye shining as it looked along the sights. He held the gun into his shoulder. For a moment he was still. Then he fired his shot. There was very little noise in the room, but the sound of broken glass from the window across the road. At that moment Holmes jumped on to his back, and threw him flat upon his face. He was up again in a moment and held Holmes by the neck, but I struck him on the head with my gun and he dropped again to the floor. I fell upon him and held him, and Holmes gave a loud call. There was the sound of running feet outside and two policemen, with a plain clothes detective, rushed through the front door and into the room.

"That you, Lestrade?" asked Holmes.

"Yes, Mr. Holmes. I took the job myself. It's good to see you back in London, sir."

■noiselessly 副 音を立てずに　■drop to ～まで（身を）沈める　■sort of ～の一種　■bend down かがみこむ　■rest 動 ～を置く　■fire one's shot 発砲する　■jump on to ～の上に飛び乗る　■throw someone flat upon one's face （人）をうつ伏せに投げつ

彼は私たちのすぐ傍を通りすぎると、窓に近づき、音をたてずに半フィートほど引き上げた。彼がこの隙間の高さまで身を沈めた時、通りの灯りがまともに彼の顔を照らした。彼はその手に、杖のようなものを手にしていた。それから彼はコートから重そうな物体を取り出し、杖とその物体を並べて置いた。彼が身体を起こした時、私は彼の手にあるのが銃の類であるとわかった。彼は銃尾を開くと何かを詰め、閉めた。そしてしゃがみこんで、開けた窓の桟の上に銃身の先を据えた。照準をのぞく彼の目が光るのがわかった。彼は銃を肩にかけ、しばらく静止し、そして発砲した。部屋にはほとんど音がしなかったが、道路の向こう側の窓ガラスが砕ける音が通りに響き渡った。その瞬間、ホームズが男の背中にとびかかり、顔を叩きつけた。男はすぐに立ち上がってホームズの首をつかんだが、私が拳銃で彼の頭を殴ると、再び床に倒れた。私は馬乗りになって男を押さえつけると、ホームズは呼び子を高々と鳴らした。外を駆けてくる足音が聞こえ、2人の警察官と私服刑事がひとり、正面の扉から部屋になだれ込んできた。

「君、レストレード君か?」とホームズが尋ねた。

「ええ、ホームズさん。自分でこの仕事を請けたのです。ロンドンにもどられて嬉しく思います」

ける ■hold someone by the neck (人)の首をつかむ ■strike someone on the head (人)の頭を殴る ■fall upon ～の上にかかる ■take the job oneself 仕事を引き受ける

We had all risen to our feet and I was able at last to get a good look at our prisoner. It was a very strong, dangerous-looking face which was turned toward us. He took no notice of any of us, but kept his eyes fixed upon Holmes's face with a look in which deep dislike and wonder showed equally. "You are too clever," he kept on saying, "far too clever!"

"Colonel," said Holmes, "I don't think I have had the pleasure of seeing you since you tried to kill me as I lay on the mountain above the Reichenbach Fall."

The colonel still stared at my friend like a man unable to believe what had happened. "You have not met Colonel Sebastian Moran, have you gentlemen," said Holmes, "once of the British Army, and one of the best shots that our country has produced. I am surprised that my very simple plan could fool an old soldier like yourself!"

Colonel Moran jumped forward with an angry shout, but the policemen held him back.

"I must say," continued Holmes, "you had one small surprise for me. I did not think that you would yourself make use of this empty house and this very window. I had thought you would work from the street, where my friend Lestrade and his men were awaiting you. With that exception all has gone as I expected."

■rise to one's feet 立ち上がる　■get a good look at ～をよく見る　■prisoner 图 拘束された人　■take no notice of ～に目もくれない　■dislike 图 嫌悪　■wonder 图 驚嘆　■colonel 图 大佐　■have the pleasure of seeing （人）にお目にかかる　■shot 图 射手　■hold someone back 引き離す　■make use of ～を使用する　■exception 图 例外

　私たちは皆立ちあがり、私はようやく、捕まえた男をよく見ることができた。屈強でいかにも凶悪な顔がこちらを向いていた。彼は他の誰にも注目せず、ただホームズの顔をじっと見ていた。その目には、深い憎悪と驚愕が同じくらいの割合で表れていた。「お前は賢すぎる」。彼は言葉をつづけた。「ずる賢いんだ」

　「大佐」とホームズが言った。「僕がライヘンバッハの滝の上の岩棚に寝そべっていた時、あなたに殺されそうになって以来ですね。こうしてお会いするのは」

　大佐はまだ、何が起こったか理解できないような面持ちで我が友をにらみつけていた。「皆さん、セバスチャン・モラン大佐にお会いになったことはないでしょう。こちらがそのお方です」とホームズは言った。「かつてイギリス陸軍に所属し、我が国が輩出した最優秀射撃者に数えられる人物です。私のごく単純な計画で、あなたのような老練な戦士をだますことができたとは驚きであります」

　モラン大佐は怒りの叫び声をあげてとびかかろうとしたが、警官たちが彼を押し戻した。

　「実は、あなたは僕にひとつの小さな驚きをもたらした」とホームズは続けた。「あなた自身がこの空家とこの窓を利用するとは思っていなかったよ。通りから仕事をすると踏んでいた。そこでは友人のレストレード君と仲間が大佐を待っていたんだ。この点以外は、全ては僕の予想した通りになった」

Colonel Moran turned to Lestrade.

"You may or may not have just cause for holding me," said he, "but at least there can be no reason why I should listen any further to what he has to say. If I am in the hands of the law, let things be done in a lawful way."

"Well, that's reasonable enough," said Lestrade. "Nothing else you have to say, Mr. Holmes, before we go?"

Holmes had picked up the powerful air gun from the floor and was looking at how it worked.

"A strange gun this, none like it," said he. "Noiseless and yet of considerable power. I knew Von Herder, the blind German doctor, who built it to the order of the late Professor Moriaty. For years I have been aware of it, though I have never before had the chance to hold it. I ask you to note it well, Lestrade, and also the bullets which fit it."

"You can trust us to look after that, Mr. Holmes," said Lestrade, as the whole group moved toward the door. "Anything further to say?"

"Only to ask what charge you will make against the colonel."

"What charge, sir? Why, of course, the attempted murder of Sherlock Holmes."

■in the hands of the law 法の適用を受ける　■lawful 形 法によって認められた
■reasonable 形 合理的な、妥当な　■noiseless 形 音のしない　■considerable 形 相当
な　■order 名 発注　■fit 動 適合する　■look after ～に気を配る　■charge 名 容疑

モラン大佐はレストレード刑事の方を向いた。

「私を逮捕する正当な理由があるかどうかは知らん」と彼は言った。「だが、少なくとも、私がこいつの話をこれ以上聞かなくてはならない理由はない。私が法の手にあるとしたら、法的なやり方で事を進めてくれ」

「なるほど、ごもっともです」とレストレードは言った。「ホームズさん、連行する前に、ほかにおっしゃりたいことはありませんか?」

ホームズは床から強力な空気銃を拾い上げ、その仕組みを調べていた。

「これは珍しい、ちょっとない銃だ」と彼は言った。「無音ながら抜群の威力をもつ。フォン・ヘルダー、故モリアーティ教授の依頼でこれを作った盲目のドイツ人技師のことは聞いていたよ。何年も前から、僕はこの銃の存在を知っていた。ただ、実物を手にしたことはなかったけれどね。レストレード君、この銃と、この特製銃弾を大切に保管するようお願いしたい」

「責任をもってお預かりします、ホームズさん」とレストレード刑事は言い、一団は扉の方へと移動していった。「何かほかに、おっしゃりたいことがあれば」

「ひとつだけ。大佐をどんな容疑で告発するのか教えてくれないか」

「どんな容疑ですと? それはもちろん、シャーロック・ホームズ氏の殺人未遂罪です」

"Not so, Lestrade. I will not appear in the matter at all. You, and you alone, will be famous for this remarkable piece of police work. Yes, Lestrade, you have done well! With your usual method of planning and nerve, you have got him."

"Got him! Got whom, Mr. Holmes?"

"The man that the whole police force has been looking for— Colonel Sebastian Moran, the man who shot the Honorable Ronald Adair with an expanding bullet from an air gun through the open window of the second floor front of No. 427 Park Lane, upon the thirtieth of last month. That's the charge, Lestrade. And now, Watson, if you can stand the cold wind from a broken window, I think that half an hour in my study over a cigarette may be of interest to you."

Our old rooms had been left unchanged on the orders of Mycroft Holmes. Mrs. Hudson smiled broadly at us both as we entered and I saw at once the strange reproduction which had played so important a part in the evening's adventure. The likeness to Holmes was almost perfect. However, part of it had been destroyed by the expanding bullet which had passed through the head, hitting the wall behind. I picked it up from the floor.

■police force 警察部隊　■be of interest to ～にとって興味深い　■be left unchanged 据え置かれる　■on the order of ～の指示で　■smile broadly 満面に笑みを浮かべる

「レストレード君、それは違う。僕はこの事件では表に出るつもりは全くない。君一人がこの逮捕劇で名を遺すんだ。そうさ、レストレード君、よくやった。君は持ち前の、入念な準備と大胆な行動力で彼を逮捕したんだ」

「彼を逮捕した? 誰を逮捕したのですか、ホームズさん」
「警察当局が全力をあげて探していた男、セバスチャン・モラン大佐、先月の30日に、ロナルド・アデア卿をパークレーン427番地三階正面の開いた窓越しに、空気銃を使って拡張弾で撃った男だ。レストレード君、これが罪状だよ。さあ、ワトスン君、もし割れた窓から吹き込む冷たい風に耐えられるのなら、僕の書斎で葉巻とともに30分ほど過ごすのは、君にとってなかなか興味深い時間になると思うがね」

私たちがかつて住んでいた部屋は、マイクロフト・ホームズの指示により、昔と変わらぬ状態に保たれていた。私たちが部屋に入ると、ハドソン夫人が私たちそれぞれににっこりとほほ笑んでくれた。そして私はそこで、今夜の冒険で重大な役割を果たした奇妙な人形を見た。ホームズに瓜二つの人形はほとんど完璧な状態だったが、拡張弾による損傷は残っていた。弾は頭を貫通して後ろの壁にぶつかっていた。私はそれを床から拾いあげた。

"A soft bullet, as you see, Watson. Very clever, who would expect to find such a thing fired from an air gun? All right, Mrs. Hudson. Thank you so much for your help. And now, Watson, let me see you in your old seat once more, for there are several points which I would like to go over with you."

I sat down and Holmes continued.

"The old hunter had not lost his nerve, nor his clear sight," said he, with a laugh, as he looked at the hole in the bust. "Right in the middle of the back of the head. He was the best shot in the army, and I expect there are few better in London. Have you heard the name?"

"No, I have not."

"Well, well! But then I remember that you had not heard the name of Professor Moriaty, one of the best minds of the century. Anyway, Colonel Moran appeared to have a record of honor as a soldier. It is true that up to a point he did well and there are many stories still told about his actions. For some reason, however, Colonel Moran began to go wrong. Without any reported trouble, he was asked to leave India. He left the army, came to London, and once more gained a bad name. It was at this time that he was found by Professor Moriaty, in whose group he was second only to Moriaty himself.

■go over ～ with ～を（人）と一緒に復習する　■sight 图 視力　■bust 图 胸像　■right in the middle of ～のど真ん中　■honor 图 名誉　■up to a point ある程度まで　■go wrong （物事が）誤った方向に進む　■second only to ～に次いで２番目

「ワトソン君、見てのとおりの柔頭銃弾だ。実に賢いね。誰がこのようなものが空気銃から発射されたと思うだろうか。ああ、もう結構です、ハドソンさん。ご協力に感謝いたします。さあ、ワトソン君、君が以前の指定席に座る姿をもう一度見せてくれないか。君と確認しておきたい点がいくつかある」

私は椅子に座り、ホームズが続けた。
「あの年老いた射手は、神経も視力も現役だ」と、人形に開いた穴を見ながら笑って言った。「後頭部の真ん中だ。軍では最高の射手だっただろう。ロンドンでも彼を超えるスナイパーはそうはいまい。彼の名前を聞いたことがあるか？」

「いや、ない」
「まあ、そうかもしれない。だが、たしか君は、今世紀最高の頭脳をもつ人物のひとりであるモリアーティ教授の名前も聞いたことがないと言っていたな。ともかく、モラン大佐は軍人としては名誉ある伝説の人物のようだよ。ある時点まではうまくいっていた。彼の功績については未だに語りつがれているよ。でも、何らかの理由で、悪い方向へ向かい始めた。公にされた問題はないものの、インドを離れることを余儀なくされた。そして退役してロンドンに戻ってきて、再び悪名を得た。モリアーティ教授に見出されたのはこの時さ。彼はこの一味で、モリアーティ教授に次ぐポジションについた。

Moriaty supplied him with money, and only used him in one or two very high-class jobs, which no normal criminal could have undertaken. You may recall the death of Mrs. Stewart in 1887. No? Well, I am sure Moran was at the bottom of it, but nothing could be proved. So cleverly was the colonel placed that, even when the Moriaty group was broken up, we could find no evidence against him. You remember at that date, when I called upon you in your rooms, how I would not stand in front of a window for fear of air guns? No doubt you thought me foolish. I knew, however, of that gun and that one of the best shots in the world would be behind it. When we were in Switzerland he followed us with Moriaty, and it was undoubtedly he who gave me that bad five minutes on the Reichenbach mountain.

"I read the papers carefully during my stay in France, on the lookout for any chance of catching him. So long as he was free in London, my life would really not have been worth living. Night and day he would have been looking for me, and sooner or later his chance must have come. What could I do? I could not kill him on sight or I would myself have been charged with murder. So I could do nothing. But I watched the criminal news, knowing that sooner or later I should get him. Then came the death of this Ronald Adair. My chance had come at last. Knowing what I did, was it not clear that Colonel Moran had done it?

■undertake 動 引き受ける　■at the bottom of ～の底辺に　■prove 動（～であることを）証明する　■cleverly 副 利口に、如才なく　■call upon ～（人）を訪問する　■for fear of ～を恐れて　■Switzerland 名 スイス　■undoubtedly 副 疑いようもなく

182

モリアーティは彼に金を与え、一つ二つの、普通の犯罪者では請け負えないような極めて高度な仕事だけを与えた。君は1887年のスチュワート夫人の死を憶えているだろうか。憶えていない？　ああ、僕は、モランが手を引いていたと確信している。でも、証明できるものは何もない。大佐は実に巧妙に身を隠していたので、モリアーティの一味が壊滅されたときでさえ、彼についての証拠を見つけることはできなかった。僕が君の部屋を訪ねた時、空気銃を恐れて窓の前に立とうとしなかった時のことを憶えているだろう。なんてばかなことを考えているんだと思っただろうね。けれども、僕は、この銃があるということと、その後ろには世界最高の射手がいるということを知っていた。僕たちがスイスにいた時、彼はモリアーティと一緒に後をつけてきた。そして、ライヘンバッハの岩棚で、僕に最悪の5分間をもたらしたのが彼であることは間違いない。

　フランスに滞在中、僕は新聞を丹念にチェックして、彼を捕まえる機会をうかがっていたんだ。彼がロンドンで自由にしている限り、僕の人生は本当の意味で生きる価値がないものになる。日夜、彼は僕を追い、遅かれ早かれチャンスを手にするはずだ。僕に何ができるだろう。彼を見つけて殺すことはできない。そんなことをしたら僕自身が殺人罪で起訴される。結局、どうすることもできなかった。それでも、いずれ彼を捕まえなければということはわかっていたから、犯罪のニュースをチェックしていた。その時、このロナルド・アデア卿死亡のニュースを知った。ついに僕にチャンスがやってきた。これまでの経緯を踏まえれば、モラン大佐がこれをやったということは確実だろうと思ったよ。

■on the lookout for　〜に目を光らせて　■so long as　〜する限り　■on sight　その場で　■be charged with　〜の罪で告発される

He had played cards with the young man, had followed him home from the club, and had shot him through the open window. There was no doubt of it. The bullets alone are enough to prove it. I came over at once, was seen by the guard, who would, I knew, tell the colonel of my presence. He could not fail to realize that my sudden return was because of his crime. I was sure that he would make an attempt to get me out of the way at once, and would bring round his murderous gun for that purpose. I left him a good mark in the window, and, having told the police that they might be needed—by the way, Watson, you spotted their presence in that doorway—I took up what seemed to me to be a wise position to watch from, never dreaming that he would choose the same spot for his attempt on my life. Now, my dear Watson, does that leave anything to explain?"

"Yes," said I. "You have not made it clear what was Colonel Moran's motive in murdering the Honorable Ronald Adair?"

"My dear Watson, there we must guess, and even a clear mind may get it wrong. Each may form his own answer given the evidence, and yours is as likely to be right as mine."

"You have formed one then?"

■open window 開いた窓　■make an attempt to ～しようと試みる　■get someone out of the way（人）に煩わされることがないように手を打つ　■bring round 持って来る　■murderous 形 殺人的な　■purpose 名 目的　■mark 名 標的　■spot 動 ～に気付く

彼はこの青年とカードをして、クラブから彼の家まで後をつけ、開いた窓越しに彼を撃った。そこに疑問の余地はない。弾丸だけでも十分にこのことを証明できる。僕はすぐに戻ってきて、見張り役の男に見つかってしまった。この男が大佐に僕の存在を知らせることはわかっていた。大佐は間違いなく、僕の突然の帰還が自分の犯罪のためになされたものだということを察するだろう。すぐにでも僕を始末しようとして、あの恐ろしい銃を持ち出すことはわかっていた。僕は彼のために、窓の中に絶好の標的を用意して、警官には、協力が必要となるかもしれないと告げた。そうそうワトソン君、君は警官たちが戸口のところにいることによく気付いたね。僕は監視するのにふさわしいと思った場所についたが、彼が僕の命を奪うために同じ場所を選ぶとは夢にも思っていなかった。さあ、ワトソン君、まだ説明していないことが何かあるかな」

「ある」と私は答えた。「モラン大佐がロナルド・アデア卿を殺す動機については何も説明していないよ」

「ああ、ワトソン君。それは推測するしかない。明晰な頭脳をもってしても、間違った答えを得る可能性がある。誰でも、与えられた証拠から自身の答えを導き出すことはできる。君の出した答えも僕の答えも、正しいという可能性は同じだ」

「では、君は答えを出したのか」

■take up（場所を）取る　■never dreaming that 〜とは夢にも思わない　■attempt on someone's life 殺人未遂　■motive 图 動機　■get it wrong 間違った思い込みをする　■form 勔 〜を形づくる　■likely to be 〜である可能性がある

"I think that it is not difficult to explain the facts. It came out in evidence that Colonel Moran and young Adair had, between them, won a considerable amount of money. Now, Moran undoubtedly played unfairly—of that I have long known. I believe that on the day of the murder Adair had found out that Moran was not playing by the rules. Very likely he had spoken to him man to man, and had said that he would tell all unless Moran gave up his membership of the club, and promised not to play cards again. Not being able to play cards, however, would be the end of Moran, who lived by his card-gains. He therefore murdered Adair, who at the time was trying to work out how much money he should himself return, since he would not make money from his playing companion's unfair play. He locked the door so that the ladies should not surprise him and ask what he was doing with those names and the money. What do you think?"

"I have no doubt that you have hit upon the truth."

"It will be proved so or not at the trial. Meanwhile, come what may, Colonel Moran will trouble us no more. The famous air gun of Von Herder will be kept by the police, and once again Mr. Sherlock Holmes is free to spend his life investigating those interesting little problems which London so readily presents."

■unfairly 副 不当に　■have long known 以前から分かっていた　■very likely たぶん、十中八九　■man to man 1対1で　■unless 腰 ～でない限り　■card-gain カードによる利益　■work out 算出する　■hit upon 思い当たる、念頭に浮かぶ　■meanwhile 副 その一方で　■readily 形 快く、喜んで

　「事実を説明することなら難しくないと思う。僕の答えは、モラン大佐とアデア卿が、ふたりしてかなりの大金を手にしたというデータに基づいたものだ。だが、モランは間違いなくいかさまをしていた——僕はずっと前からそのことに気付いていた。アデア卿は、あの日、モランが不正をしているのを見つけたのだと思う。彼がモランと一対一で話をし、モランがクラブを辞め、二度とカードをやらないと約束しない限り、このことを公にすると告げたことは十分に考えられる。　しかし、カードができないということは、これで生計をたてていたモランにとっては終わりを意味する。それで彼はアデア卿を殺害した。殺されたとき、アデア卿は、仲間の不正で儲けるわけにはいかないからと、自分はどれだけの金を返さなくてはならないかを計算しようとしていたのだろう。扉に鍵をかけたのは、母親や妹が突然入ってきて、名前と金を見て何をしているのかと聞かれることがないように用心したのさ。これでどうかな」

　「君は明らかに真実を言い当てたと思うよ」
　「真実かどうかは裁判でわかるだろう。ともかく、どんな結果が出るとしても、僕らはもう、モラン大佐に煩わされることはない。フォン・ヘルダーの例の空気銃は、警察に保管されている。かくしてシャーロック・ホームズ氏は、再び自由を得て、ロンドンが気前よく与えてくれるちょっとした興味深い事件の調査に人生を捧げることができるようになったというわけだ」

覚えておきたい英語表現

May I ask how you knew where to find me? （p.144, 8行目）

どうしてここがわかったのですか？

【解説】

May I ask 〜は、〜について尋ねるときの、丁寧な表現です。「〜について尋ねても
よろしいでしょうか？」というニュアンスになります。聞きづらいことを尋ねるとき
にも使える、"気くばり表現" です。Do you mind if I ask you 〜も、「〜についてお
尋ねしてもよろしいでしょうか？」という意味で、よく使われています。直訳すると、
「〜についてお尋ねしても、お気を悪くされませんでしょうか？」

【例文】① May I ask how old you are?
お歳をお尋ねしてもよろしいでしょうか？

② May I ask if you are married?
ご結婚されていらっしゃるかどうか、お聞きしてもよろしいですか？

You can trust us to look after that. （p.176, 下から6行目）

責任をもってお預かりします。

【解説】trust は、「信用する、信頼する」という意味です。trust は、relationship（人
間関係）において不可欠です。to look after 〜 は、「〜の世話をする、管理する」と
いう意味で、対象は、人や物などさまざまです。文中では、銃を指しているので、訳
文では、「お預かりします」となっています。

【例文】① Life is about who you trust.
人生とは、誰を信用するかにつきる。

＊深い言葉です。「人の幸せは、誰を信用するのかによって左右される」という意味です。
人間は日々、誰（何）かを信用して選択しています。学校や会社選び、友だちやパート
ナーの選択、食べ物や薬、服や住む家等、ブランドや広告、口コミや見かけ、経験など
を信頼して、選択しているのです。でも、時には、その信頼が裏切られることもありま
す。真に信頼できる相手や対象を見極め、幸福を招く、賢い選択をしましょう。

② My sister looks after our parents.
妹は両親の面倒を見てくれています。

You spotted their presence in that doorway. （p.184, 10行目）
君は彼ら（警官たち）が戸口のところにいることによく気付いたね。

【解説】spotは、「見つける、見抜く、突きとめる」という意味の動詞です。presence
は、「存在、存在感」という意味です。

【例文】① Your presence today matters to me very much.
あなたが今日いらしてくださったことは、私にとって、とても大切なことです。

② We wish to have a presence in the European market.
欧州市場に参入したいと願います。

Does that leave anything to explain? （p.184, 下から8行目）
まだ説明していないことが何かあるかな？

【解説】leave 〜 to explainは、「説明を要する〜が残る」という意味です。

【例文】① Now, it leaves only one thing to explain.
さて、説明すべきことはあと一つだけとなった。

② It leaves nothing more to show you.
これで、すべてをお見せしました。

Each may form his own answer given the evidence, and yours
is as likely to be right as mine. （p.184, 下から3行目）
誰でも、与えられた証拠から自身の答えを導き出すことはできる。君の
出した答えも僕の答えも、正しいという可能性は同じだ。

【解説】evidence（証拠）は一つでも、そこから導き出される答えは、人によってさま
ざまだという、ホームズの鋭い指摘です。
as likely to be right as 〜 は、「〜同様、正しいだろう」という意味です。

【例文】① Each may interpret the evidence in his own way.
各自が証拠を好きなように解釈するだろう。

② It is likely to rain tomorrow.
明日はおそらく雨だろう。

189

THE

OF THE

踊る人形

ADVENTURE DANCING MAN

ホームズは奇妙な人形の絵が続く紙切れに見入っていた。
今日の依頼者の妻はこれを見て死ぬほど怖がっているという。
これにはどんな謎が隠されているのだろう……

ドイルがホームズ物語を書いたのは
まだ探偵小説（推理小説）が書かれはじめたころであり、
その先駆者エドガー・アラン・ポー（1809–1849）の影響を
強く受けている。『ボヘミアの醜聞』は
ポーの『盗まれた手紙』のアイディアを流用しているし、
『まだらの紐』の動物が殺人の手段というのも
『モルグ街の殺人』からヒントを得たのかもしれない。
『踊る人形』の暗号の解読法はポーの『黄金虫』と同じである。

しかしドイルはポーのアイディアを違う世界におきかえて、
素晴らしい作品に仕立てなおしているのだ。
ホームズ物語にはこれ以後の推理小説のトリックの
ほとんどすべての原型があるといわれている。

The Adventure of the Dancing Man

Holmes had been seated for some hours quietly working at his papers.

"So, Watson," said he suddenly, "you are not going to put money into that South African company?"

I gave a start of surprise. Although I was used to Holmes's clever mind, this sudden insight into my deep thoughts was not possible to explain.

"How on earth do you know that?" I asked.

He turned round with laughter in his deep-set eyes.

"Now, Watson, say you are completely taken aback," said he.

"I am."

"I ought to make you sign a paper saying that."

"Why?"

■put money into ～に出資する　■give a start of surprise　驚いてビクッとする
■insight 名 洞察力、眼識　■How on earth 一体どうやったら～　■deep-set 形 深くくぼんだ　■taken aback ～にびっくりさせられる　■ought to ～すべきである

踊る人形

ホームズは何時間も黙って座ったまま、手元の書類を読んでいた。

「それでワトソン君」と突然口を開いたかと思うと、「君は南アフリカの会社への投資をやめたんだね」と言い出した。

私は驚いてビクッとした。ホームズの鋭さには慣れてはいるものの、どうしてこんな風に突然に私の考えていることを読み取ることができるのか、全くわからない。

「いったいどうしてわかったんだ?」

ホームズはこちらを向いた。深くくぼんだ目に笑みが浮かんでいる。

「ああワトソン君、不意をつかれて驚いただろうね」

「そうだね」

「今の言葉を書面にして、署名しておいてもらわなくてはならないな」

「どうして?」

"Because in five minutes you will say that it is all so very simple."

"I am sure I will say nothing of the kind."

"You see, my dear Watson, it is not really difficult to take a set of ideas, each subject to the one before and each simple in itself. If, after doing so, one simply removes all the ideas in the middle and gives the listener the starting point and the end result, one may produce a surprised reaction. Now it was not really difficult by looking at your left forefinger and thumb to be sure that you were not going to put your money in the gold fields."

"I see no connection."

"Very likely not; but I can quickly show you a close connection. Here are the missing ideas of this very simple piece of reasoning: 1. You had chalk on your left forefinger and thumb when you returned from the club last night. 2. You get chalk there when you play billiards. 3. You only play billiards with Thurston. 4. You told me, four weeks ago, that Thurston wanted to buy some South African land, which he wished you to share with him, and that you only had a month to decide. 5. Your bank book is locked in my cupboard and you have not asked for the key. 6. You have decided not to put your money into this plan."

"How very simple!" I cried.

■nothing of the kind 決してそうでない　■one 代 人　■starting point 出発点
■end result 結末　■reaction 名 反応　■forefinger 名 人さし指　■thumb 名 親指
■gold field 金鉱地　■connection 名 関係、つながり　■Very likely not. 「おそらくそ
うだろう」　■chalk 名 チョーク　■billiard 名 ビリヤード　■share with （人）と共有す
る　■cupboard 名 戸棚

194

「5分後には、君は『まったく単純な話だ』と言うだろうから」

「そんなことは言わないよ」

「ねぇ、ワトソン君、情報が一揃いあって、ひとつひとつを順につなげ、それぞれを単純に考えるということはそれほど難しいことではないよ。そのようにしてから核心部分を中心から取り除き、始まりと終わりを聞かせてやると、相手は驚くわけだ。まぁ、君の左手の人差し指と親指を見れば、君が金鉱への投資をやめたに違いないということは容易にわかるよ」

「僕にはどうしてそのふたつがつながるのかわからないけれど」

「当然だろう。でも、僕はその深いつながりを手短に説明することができる。そこにはごく単純な論理のつながりの失われた一片があるんだ。1．君が昨夜、クラブから帰ってきた時、君の人差し指と親指にチョークの粉がついていた。2．君はビリヤードをするとき、その部分にチョークをつける。3．君がビリヤードをするのは、サーストンとだけだ。4．4週間前、君は、サーストンがある南アフリカの土地を君と共同で購入したがっていて、1ヵ月以内にどうするか決めなくてはならないと言っていた。5．君の通帳は僕の鍵のついた戸棚の中にあるけれど、君はその鍵を要求してこなかった。6．君はこの話に投資するのをやめた」

「なんて単純な話なんだ!」と私は叫んだ。

"Quite so!" said he, rather quickly. "Every problem becomes very easy when it is explained to you. Here is an unexplained one. See what you can make of that, friend Watson." He threw a piece of paper upon the table, and turned once more to his work.

I looked with surprise at the marks on the paper. "Why, Holmes, it is a child's picture," I cried.

"That's your idea, isn't it?"

"What else could it be?"

"That is what Mr. Hilton Cubitt, of Riding Thorpe Manor, Norfolk, wants to know. This little problem came by the first mail, and he was to follow by the next train. There's a ring at the bell, Watson. I think this will be him."

A heavy step was heard upon the stairs, and a moment later there entered a tall, healthy looking gentleman, whose clear eyes and red face told of a life led far from the smoke of Baker Street. He seemed to bring a smell of fresh country air with him as he entered. Having shaken hands with each of us, he was about to sit down, when he saw the paper with the strange markings which I had looked at, upon the table.

"Well, Mr. Holmes, what do you make of these?" he cried. "They told me that you liked strange mysteries, and I don't think you can find a stranger one than that. I sent the paper on ahead, so that you might have time to study it before I came."

■unexplained 形 解明されていない　■what you can make of ～をどう考えられるか
■Riding Thorpe Manor ライディング・ソープ荘園《日本語版では一般に「リドリング・ソープ」（Ridling Thorpe）としていますが、英文は底本のBantam版に従っています》

「その通りだよ」と、ホームズはぴしゃりと言った。「どんな問題も、説明してしまえば簡単なんだ。でも、ここにまだ解けない問題がある。ワトソン君、君はこれをどう思う?」 ホームズは、一枚の紙をテーブルの上に放り出して、また机に向かった。

　私はその紙に書かれた絵を見て驚いた。「なんだよ、ホームズ、子どもの落書きか」

　「君はそう思うのか」

　「ほかに何がある?」

　「それをノーフォーク州リドリング・ソープ荘園のヒルトン・キュービット氏が知りたがっているんだ。この謎の問題が今朝の最初の郵便で届いた。そして彼がその次の列車で来ることになっている。ベルが鳴ったね。ワトソン君、彼が来たんだろう」

　重い足音が階段に響いたかと思うと、背の高い、いかにも健康そうな紳士が入ってきた。その澄んだ目と血色のよい顔は、ベイカー街の霧とは無縁のところで暮らす人物であることを物語っていた。入ってきたときには、彼の周りからさわやかな田園の香りが漂ってくるようだった。彼は私たちふたりと握手を交わし、腰を下ろそうとして、テーブルの上の奇妙な絵が書かれた紙に目をとめた。先ほど私が見ていたものだ。

　「ああホームズさん、これをどう思われます?」と氏は悲痛ともいえる声をあげた。「あなたは変わった謎がお好きだと伺いましたが、これより変わったものをご覧になったことはないのではないでしょうか。私がこちらに伺う前にお考えになるかと思って、前もってお送りしたのです」

■Norfolk 図 ノーフォーク州　■a ring at the bell 呼び鈴の音　■there 副 そこに
■tell of 〜について話す［説明する］　■each of 〜のそれぞれ　■marking 図 マーク、印
■on ahead 前もって、事前に

"It is clearly rather unusual," said Holmes. "At first sight it would appear to be a children's game. It is a number of strange little figures dancing across the paper. Why should you put any importance on something so seemingly meaningless?"

"I never should, Mr. Holmes. But my wife does. For some reason she is afraid of it. She says nothing but I can see the fear in her eyes. That is why I must get to the bottom of this matter."

Holmes held up the paper to the light. It was a page taken from a notebook. The markings were like this:

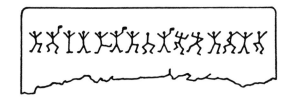

Holmes looked at it for some time and then put it carefully in his pocket book.

"This promises to be a most interesting and unusual case," said he. "You gave me a few facts in your letter, Mr. Hilton Cubitt, but I would like you to go over it all again for my friend, Dr. Watson."

■at first sight 一見したところでは ■put importance on ～を重要視する
■seemingly 副 一見したところ ■meaningless 形 無意味な ■for some reason どうしたわけか ■fear 名 恐怖 ■get to the bottom of（事件などの）真相を探る ■hold up 持ち上げる ■pocket book 手帳 ■go over ～を繰り返し行う

「たしかに、いささか変わっていますね」とホームズは答えた。「ちょっと見たところでは、子どものいたずらのように見えます。奇妙な小さい人形が、紙の上を並んで踊っているみたいだ。なぜ、このような他愛なく見える代物を重く受け止めていらっしゃるのでしょうか」

「私ではないのですよ、ホームズさん。私の妻なのです。何か理由があって、これを怖がっているのです。彼女は何も言いませんが、目に恐怖の色が浮かんでいるのがわかります。ですから、私はこの件を徹底的に調べなくてはと思ったのです」

ホームズは紙きれを取り上げ、光に透かしてみた。メモ帳から破りとったもので、次のような絵が描かれていた。

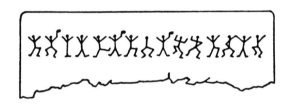

ホームズはしばらくの間それを眺めてから、大切そうに手帳に挟んだ。

「これは実に興味深い、珍しい事件になりそうですね」とホームズは言った。「ヒルトン・キュービットさん、お手紙のなかでいくつかの情報を書いて下さいましたが、私の友人のドクター・ワトソンのためにもう一度お話しいただけないでしょうか」

"I'm not much of a storyteller," said our visitor nervously. "You'll have to ask me anything that I don't make clear. I'll begin at the time of my marriage last year, but I want to say this first of all. I'm not a rich man, but my people have been at Riding Thorpe for a matter of five centuries, and there is no better known family in Norfolk. Last year I came up for the summer, and I stopped at a boarding house in Russell Square. Parker, a friend of mine, was staying there. There was an American young lady there — Patrick was the name — Elsie Patrick. In some way we became friends, until before my month was up I was as much in love as a man could be. We were quietly married, and we returned to Norfolk as man and wife. You'll think it very mad, Mr. Holmes, that a man of a good family should marry a wife in this manner, knowing nothing of her past or of her people, but if you saw her and knew her, it would help you to understand.

"She was very straight about it, was Elsie. I can't say that she did not give me every chance of getting out of it if I wished to do so. 'I have known some bad people in my life,' said she. 'I wish to forget all about them. I would rather never talk of the past, for it is very painful for me. If you take me, Hilton, you will take a woman who has done nothing wrong herself, but you will have to be happy with me as I am now, and to allow me to say nothing about all that passed up to the time when I became yours.

■not much of a 大した〜でない ■storyteller 图 語り手 ■nervously 圖 神経質になって ■make clear はっきりさせる ■first of all まず第一に ■for a matter of 〜 centuries 約〜世紀の間 ■come up （人が）都会に出る ■boarding house 宿泊施設

200

「私は話すのが得意ではないので」と依頼人は緊張して話し始めた。「わかり
にくいところは何でもお尋ねください。昨年私が結婚した時のことから始めま
しょう。いえ、それよりもまずお話ししておきたいことがあります。私は決し
て裕福ではありませんが、実家はここ5世紀の間リドリング・ソープにあり、
ノーフォークでは一番の旧家です。昨年の夏、私はこちらに来て、ラッセル・
スクエアの宿泊所に滞在しました。友人のパーカーさんがそこに滞在していた
のです。そこにアメリカの若い女性がいました。パトリック――エルシー・
パトリックという名前でした。いろいろあって知り合いになり、休暇が終わる
ころにはこれ以上ないくらいに彼女のことを好きになっていました。私たちは
ひっそりと結婚し、夫婦としてノーフォークに帰りました。ホームズさん、旧
家の男がこんなふうに、相手の過去も家柄も知らずに結婚するなど、おかしい
と思われるでしょうね。でも、彼女に会って、彼女を知って下されば、わかっ
ていただけると思います。

　エルシーは、そのことに関してはっきりしています。私が望むのならいつ
でも結婚はとりやめるという態度で私に向かってくれました。『私には、良
くない知り合いがいます』と言いました。『その人たちのことは忘れたいの
です。過去のことは、できればお話ししたくはありません。とても辛いこと
なので。ヒルトンさん、私を受け入れて下さるなら、あなたは、その本人に
は何一つ落ち度のない女を手に入れることになるでしょう。あなたには、今
の私といて幸せだと思っていただきたいのです。そして私があなたの妻に
なる前の、過去のことを話さなくて構わないとおっしゃってほしいのです。

■up 形（期間が）終わりで　■man and wife 夫婦　■mad 形 正気でない　■in this
manner こんな具合に　■straight 形 率直な、包みかくしのない　■getting out of ～か
ら手を引く　■painful 形 苦痛な、つらい　■up to the time ～までの時

If these conditions are too hard, then go back to Norfolk, and leave me to the lonely life in which you found me.' It was the day before our marriage that she said those very words to me. I told her that I was content to take her on those conditions, and I have been as good as my word.

"Well, we have been married now for a year, and very happy we have been. But about a month ago, at the end of June, I saw, for the first time, signs of trouble. One day my wife received a letter from America. She turned deadly white, read the letter, and threw it on the fire. She said nothing about it afterwards, and neither did I, for a promise is a promise, but she has never known an easy hour from that moment. There is always a look of fear upon her face. She would do better to trust me, for she would find that I was her best friend. But until she speaks, I can say nothing. Mind you, she is an honorable woman, Mr. Holmes, and whatever trouble there may have been in her past life it has not been caused by her. I am only a simple Norfolk countryman, but there is not a man in England who holds his family honor more highly than I do. She knows it well, and she knew it well before she married me. She would never have married me if she felt she would cause a problem to my family, of that I am sure.

その条件が無理ならば、ノーフォークへお帰り下さい。私をあなたに出会った
ときの孤独な生活に戻して下さい』。これは結婚の前日に、妻が私に言った言
葉です。私は彼女に、喜んで条件を受け入れると言いました。そして、その言
葉どおりにしてきました。

　ええ、私たちはこの1年、結婚生活を続けてきました。とても幸せな生活で
した。ところが一ヵ月ほど前、6月の末に、私は初めて災いの兆しを感じまし
た。ある日、妻はアメリカからの手紙を受け取りました。妻は真っ青になり、
手紙を読むと、それを火の中に投げ込みました。その後、妻はこのことについ
て何も言いませんし、私も何も言いませんでした。約束でしたから。しかし妻
はそれ以来、気が休まる時がないようで、顔から不安の色が消えることがあり
ません。頼ってくれればいいのに。私という最高のパートナーを見つけたのだ
から、と思っていました。でも、妻から言い出すまでは、私からは何も言えま
せん。わかって下さい、ホームズさん。妻は高潔な女性なんです。過去に何か
問題があったとしても、それは妻のせいではないのです。私はノーフォークの
田舎者にすぎません。でも家名を重んじることでは、英国中のだれにも負けま
せん。そして妻もそのことをよくわかっています。結婚する前から十分にその
ことを知っていました。妻は、自分が私の実家に迷惑をかけるだろうと思って
いたら、私と結婚などしなかったでしょう。それは間違いありません。

"Well, now I come to the strange part of my story. About a week ago, I found by one of the windows a number of strange little dancing figures like these upon the paper. They were written with chalk. I thought it was the stable-boy who had done them, but he said that he knew nothing about them. Anyhow they had been put there during the night. I had them washed out and only told my wife afterwards. To my surprise, she thought it most grave, and asked me to let her see them if any more come. None did come for a week, and then yesterday morning I found this paper lying on the sunclock in the garden. I showed it to Elsie, and she passed out in front of me. Since then she has looked like a woman in a dream, with fear always in her eyes. It was then that I wrote and sent the paper to you, Mr. Holmes. It was not a thing I could take to the police, for they would have laughed at me, but you will tell me what to do. I am not a rich man but if there is any danger to my little woman, I would spend my last shilling to save her."

He was a fine man, this son of the English soil—simple, straight, and gentle, with his true blue eyes and broad, friendly face. His love for his wife and his trust in her was written on his face. Holmes had listened to his story very carefully, and now he sat for some time quietly thinking.

"Don't you think, Mr. Cubitt," said he at last, "that your best plan would be to directly question your wife, and ask her to share her story with you?"

■by 副 そばに、傍らに　■stable-boy 图 馬番の少年　■anyhow 副 とにかく　■wash out 洗い落とす　■sunclock 图 日時計　■shilling 图 シリング《貨幣単位》　■son of the soil 土地の人　■broad 形 （幅が）広い

さて、いよいよ奇妙な箇所に入ります。1週間ほど前、私は窓のひとつに、この紙に書かれているような、奇妙で小さな踊る人形がいくつか描かれているのを見つけました。チョークで描かれていました。馬番の少年が描いたのだと思ったのですが、彼は何も知らないと言います。とにかく、夜のうちに描かれたものでした。私はその落書きを洗い流させてから、妻に話しました。驚いたことに、妻はひどく深刻に受け止めて、またこのようなことがあったら見せてほしいと言うのです。それから1週間は何もありませんでしたが、昨日の朝、庭の日時計の上にこの紙が置かれているのを見つけました。それを見せると、妻はその場で倒れてしまいました。それ以来、妻は心ここに在らずという表情で、目には恐怖が浮かんでいます。それから私はホームズさんに手紙を書き、この紙をお送りしました。警察に届けるわけにもいきません。だって、笑われるだけでしょう。でも、あなたなら、どうしたらいいかを教えて下さると思ったのです。私は裕福ではありませんが、愛する女性に危険が迫っているとしたら、全財産をかけても守るつもりです」

善人だ。素朴でまっすぐで、温かい、古き善きイギリス人そのものである。実直さがあふれる青い目と人のよさそうな広い顔には、妻への愛と信頼があふれていた。ホームズは彼の話に耳を傾け、それからしばらく黙って考え込んだ。

そしてやっと口を開くと言った。「キュービットさん、一番いいのは奥様に率直にお聞きになって、秘密を打ち明けてもらうことではないでしょうか」

Hilton Cubitt looked down.

"A promise is a promise, Mr. Holmes. If Elsie wished to tell me, she would. If not, it is not for me to make her. But I must try in some way to help her, and I will."

"Then I will help you with all my heart. In the first place have you heard of any strangers being seen around Riding Thorpe?"

"No."

"I suppose that it is a very quiet place. Any fresh face would be noticed?"

"Around Riding Thorpe Manor, yes. But we have several small watering places not very far away. And the farmers take in people."

"These markings clearly have a meaning. If it is, as I think, a system, I have no doubt that we shall get to the bottom of it. But there are not enough figures in this set to be able to work anything out, and the facts that you bring me give us nothing with which to start an investigation. I would suggest that you return to Norfolk, that you keep a lookout, and that you take a careful copy of any fresh dancing men that may appear. Ask people whether any strangers have been seen in the area. When you have got some fresh evidence, come to me again. That is the best thing that you can do, Mr. Hilton Cubitt. If necessary, I shall always be ready to run down and see you in your Norfolk home."

■It is not for me to 私が～することではない　■with all one's heart 真心を込めて
■fresh 形 新たな　■watering place 海岸のリゾート地　■take in （客を）迎え入れる、泊める　■work out （謎・暗号が）解ける　■keep a lookout 警戒する　■run down 駆けつける

　ヒルトン・キュービット氏は視線を落とした。

　「ホームズさん、約束は約束です。妻が話したいと思うなら、話してくれるでしょう。話したくないなら、無理強いしたくはない。でも、なんとかして妻の力になりたい。なるつもりです」

　「そういうことなら喜んで力になりましょう。まず、リドリング・ソープの近くに不審な人物がいるという話をお聞きになったことはありませんか?」

　「ありません」

　「閑静なところのようですが、新顔がやってきていませんか?」

　「荘園付近にはやってきます。すぐ近くに小さな海水浴場がありますから、農家が人を泊めているのです」

　「この記号には、明らかに意味があります。私の予測が当たっていて、ここに決まりがあるとすれば、その謎を解くことができるはずです。でも、これだけでは短すぎて何もできず、また、お話ししていただいた情報だけでは調べようがありません。ノーフォークにお戻りになってはいかがでしょう。監視を続け、この踊る人形がまた現れたら、正確に描き写しておいて下さい。見慣れない人間がうろついていなかったかどうか、周りに聞いてみて下さい。新しい証拠が手に入ったら、またいらして下さい。キュービットさん、これがあなたのできる最善の策です。必要とあれば、いつでも駆けつけます。ノーフォークのお宅でお会いしましょう」

The meeting left Sherlock Holmes very thoughtful, and several times in the next few days I saw him take the piece of paper from his notebook and look long and hard at the strange figures on it. He said nothing about it, however, until one afternoon two weeks or so later. I was going out when he called me back.

"You had better stay here, Watson."

"Why?"

"Because I had a telegram from Hilton Cubitt this morning. You remember Hilton Cubitt, of the dancing men? He was to reach Liverpool Street at one-twenty. He may be here at any moment. I gather from his telegram that there have been some new turns to this case."

We had not long to wait, for our Norfolk gentleman came straight from the station as fast as a cab could bring him. He was looking upset and unhappy with tired eyes and a lined face.

"It's getting on my nerves, this business, Mr. Holmes," said he, as he dropped into an armchair. "It's bad enough to feel that there are unknown people about you, who have some kind of plan against you, but when, in addition to that, you know that it is killing your wife by inches, then it becomes as much as a man can take. She's wearing away under it, wearing away before my eyes."

"Has she said anything yet?"

■thoughtful 形 思いにふけった ■telegram 名 電報 ■at any moment 今すぐにも ■new turn 新しい展開 ■lined face しわの寄った顔 ■get on someone's nerves (人) の神経に障る ■drop into 〜に崩れ落ちる ■unknown 形 未知の ■in addition to 〜に加えて ■by inches 少しずつ、徐々に

208

この面談ののち、シャーロック・ホームズは深くもの思いにふけった。続く数日間は、手帳から例の紙切れを取り出しては、その奇妙な人形を食い入るように見るということが幾度かあった。それでも私には何も言わずに時が過ぎたが、二週間ほどたったある日の午後、出かけようとする私を呼びとめた。

「ワトソン君、君はここにいた方がいいよ」

「どうして?」

「今朝、ヒルトン・キュービット氏から電報が届いたよ。あの踊る人形のキュービット氏だよ。憶えているだろう? 1時20分にリバプール街駅に着くことになっている。もうすぐここに来るよ。電報を見たところでは、この事件に新しい展開があったようだね」

ほどなくして、ノーフォークの紳士が全速力で走る二輪馬車に乗って、駅からまっすぐにやってきた。困憊した様子で、目には疲れの色が浮かび、顔には皺が刻まれていた。

「ホームズさん、今回はほとほと参りました」と、彼は肘掛け椅子にもたれかかった。「見知らぬ人間が何かをたくらみ、おまけに妻をじわじわと追い詰めて思い通りにしようとしていると考えてみて下さい。悲惨でしょう。妻はそんな状況におかれ、日に日に弱っていっていくのです。私の目の前で」

「奥様はまだ何もお話しにならない?」

"No, Mr. Holmes, she has not. Yet there have been times when the poor girl has wanted to speak, and yet could not quite bring herself to tell me. I have tried to help her, but I suppose I did it badly and put her off. She has spoken about my family and our name in Norfolk, and our pride in our honor, and I always felt it was leading to the point, but somehow it turned off before we got there."

"But have you found out something for yourself?"

"A good deal, Mr. Holmes. I have several fresh dancing men pictures for you to look at, and, what is more important, I have seen the fellow."

"What! The man who makes these marks?"

"Yes, I saw him doing it. But I will tell you everything in order. When I got back after my visit to you, the very first thing I saw next morning was a fresh set of dancing men. They had been drawn in chalk upon the black wooden door of the stable, which is beside the grass in full view of the front windows. I took a careful copy, and here it is." He got out a piece of paper and laid it upon the table. Here is a copy of the figures:

"Very good!" said Holmes. "Very good indeed, please continue."

■put off 気を悪くさせる、不快にする　■turn off（話を）そらす、脇道へそれる　■good deal たくさん　■in order 順番に　■get back 戻る　■stable 图 納屋　■take a copy 複写する、控えをとる　■here it is これです

210

「ええ、ホームズさん、言いません。何か言いたそうにしたことはあったのですが、話すには至りませんでした。助けようとしたのですけれど上手くいかず、黙ってしまうばかりでした。妻が私の家族、ノーフォークでの名声や、名誉を誇りに思っていることについて話すことがあり、そのたびにいよいよ本題に入るのだろうと思うのですが、その前に話が逸れてしまうのです」

「何かご自身でお気づきになったことはありませんか?」
「たくさんあります。新しい踊る人形の絵をいくつか写してきました。ご覧になっていただきたくて。さらに重要なことは、犯人を見たのです」

「なんと。この絵を描いた人物を?」
「ええ、現場を見ました。ああ、順番にお話ししましょう。先日こちらに伺って帰宅したその翌朝、また新たな踊る人形たちを見つけたのです。納屋の黒い木の扉にチョークで描かれていました。納屋は芝生を挟んで正面の窓からよく見通せるのです。間違えないように写してきました。これです」。彼は一枚の紙を取り出し、机の上に広げた。これがその絵の写しである。

「素晴らしい」とホームズが声をあげた。「実に素晴らしい。さあ、お続け下さい」

"When I had taken the copy, I removed the marks, but, two mornings later, a fresh set had appeared. I have a copy of it here":

Holmes laughed with pleasure.

"Our material is quickly increasing," said he.

"Three days later another note was left upon paper, and placed under a stone upon the sunclock. Here it is. The figures are, as you see, the same as the last group. After that I decided to lie in wait, so I got out my gun, and I sat up in my study, which overlooks the garden. About two in the morning I was seated by the window, all being dark save for the moonlight outside, when I heard steps behind me, and there was my wife. She asked me to come to bed. I told her that I wanted to see who it was that played such a strange game with us. She answered that it was all nonsense, and that I should take no notice of it.

"She asked me to come to bed but suddenly I saw her face grow whiter in the moonlight. Something was moving by the stable. I saw a dark figure low to the ground move round the corner in front of the door. Holding my gun, I was about to rush out, when my wife threw her arms around me and held me with all her strength. At last I got clear, but by the time I got into the garden the man was gone. However, on the stable door was the very same

■material 图 材料　■increasing 形 増えている　■lie in wait 待ち伏せする　■get out ～を取り出す　■overlook 動 監視する　■nonsense 图 つまらない［無駄な］こと ■take no notice of ～を気に留めない　■grow 動 ～の状態になる　■moonlight 图 月 光　■rush out 急いで出て行く　■with all one's strength 力いっぱいに

「写し取ってから、絵を消しました。でも、2日後の朝、また新しい絵が描かれていました。その写しがこれです」

ホームズは嬉しそうに笑った。

「材料が集まってきたな」

「それから3日後、紙に描かれた絵が、日時計の上にある石の下に敷かれていました。これです。ご覧のとおり、先程のと同じものです。私は待ち伏せしてやろうと思って、銃を取り出して書斎に待機し、庭を見張りました。午前2時頃、窓ぎわに腰かけていた時のことでした。外は月明かりだけで真っ暗です。背後に足音が聞こえました。妻でした。私に寝室に戻るように言うので、私は、こんな妙ないたずらをしかけた犯人を見つけたいのだと言いました。すると妻は、そんなことは意味がない、気にしてはいけないと言うのです。

妻は寝室に戻るようにと言ってきました。でも、その時突然、妻の顔が月の光に照らされて白く光るのが見えました。納屋のそばで何かが動いたのです。黒い低い影が、扉の正面に回ったのです。銃を持って飛び出そうとすると、妻は腕を私の身体に回して、全力で止めるのです。ようやく振りほどき、庭についた時には、奴の姿はありませんでした。でも、納屋の扉には、前と同じ踊る人形の絵がありました。さきほどの紙に描いたものです。庭をくまなく探しましたが、奴の痕跡はどこにも見つかりませんでした。しかし驚いたことに、奴

set of dancing men which had appeared already, and which I have copied on that paper. There was no sign of the fellow anywhere, though I ran all over the grounds. And yet the remarkable thing is that he must have been there all the time, for when I looked at the door again in the morning, he had done some more of his pictures under the line which I had already seen."

"Have you that fresh set?"

"Yes, it is very short, but I made a copy of it, and here it is."

Again he produced a paper. The new dance was in this form:

"Tell me," said Holmes, and I could see by his eyes that this was important, "was this an addition to the first or did it appear to be separate?"

"It was on a different part of the door."

"Very good! This is by far the most important of all for our purpose. It fills me with hopes. Now, Mr. Hilton Cubitt, please continue your most interesting statement."

■all over 全体にわたって　■produce 動 ～を取り出す　■form 名 形　■addition 名 付加、追加　■separate 形 別々になった　■by far 群を抜いて、圧倒的に　■statement 名 発言、供述

214

はそこにずっといたようなのです。翌朝また納屋を見てみると、昨夜描かれた
絵の下に、新しい絵がいくつか描かれていました」

「その写しをお持ちですか?」
「ええ。とても短いものですが、写してきました。これです」
彼はまた紙を取り出した。新しい踊りは次のような形だった。

「教えて下さい」とホームズが言う。彼の目をみると、重要なことだというこ
とがわかる。「最初のものに付け足されていたのでしょうか、それとも、まっ
たく別のもののようでしたか?」
「ドアの別の場所に描かれていました」
「素晴らしい。これは今までの資料の中でも群を抜いて重要なものです。希
望がもてそうですよ。さあ、ヒルトン・キュービットさん、その興味深い話を
続けて下さい」

"I have nothing more to say, Mr. Holmes, except that I was angry with my wife that night for having held me back when I might have caught the fellow. She said that she feared that I might get hurt. For a moment it had crossed my mind that perhaps what she really feared was that he might be hurt, for I could not doubt that she knew who this man was and what he meant by these strange signs. But when I looked in my wife's eyes, I was sure that it was indeed my safety that was in her mind. There's the whole case, and now I want your opinion as to what I ought to do. My own feeling is to put some of my farm boys in the garden, and when this fellow comes again, to give him such a going-over that he will leave us in peace in the future."

"I fear that it is too deep a case for such simple steps," said Holmes. "How long can you stay in London?"

"I must go back today. I would not leave my wife alone all night for anything. She is very nervous, and asked me to come back."

"I think you are right. But if you could have stopped, I might possibly have been able to return with you in a day or two. Meanwhile, you will leave me these papers, and I think that it is very likely that I shall be able to pay you a visit shortly and to throw some light upon the case."

■hold back 引き止める　■get hurt けがをする、傷つく　■what somebody means by (人) がどういう意味で〜と言っているのか　■going-over 図 (手ひどく) たたく [打つ] こと　■in peace 平安に　■fear 動 (残念なことを) 言う　■simple steps 簡単な手順　■meanwhile 副 その間に　■pay 〜 a visit 〜を訪問する

「これ以上お話しすることはないのですよ、ホームズさん。ただ、私はその夜、奴をつかまえようとするのを止めたことで妻を叱りました。妻は、私が怪我をするのが怖かったのだと言いました。一瞬、妻が本当に恐れているのは奴が怪我をすることではないかという考えが心をよぎりました。彼女はこの男の正体を知っており、彼が描く踊る人形の意味もわかっているのではないかと思いました。しかし、妻の目を見れば、彼女が案じていたのは私の身だとわかりました。これが全てです。さて、私はどうしたらいいのかご意見をお聞かせいただきたいのです。私としては、農場の少年たちを何人か庭に待機させて、奴がまたやってきたら痛めつけてやって、今後二度と私たちの生活に近寄らないようにさせようと思うのですが」

「そんな簡単なことで解決できる事件ではないように思います」とホームズは言った。「ロンドンにはいつまでいらっしゃいますか」

「今日帰らなくてはなりません。妻を一晩中ひとりにしておくことなど、考えられません。おびえてしまっていて、帰って来てくれと言うのです」

「それが賢明でしょう。ロンドンに滞在なさるなら、一両日中にはご同行できるかと思ったのですが。ともかく、この紙はお預かりしていいでしょうか。近々お訪ねして、この事件にいくらかの光明を投げかけることができるかと思います」

Sherlock Holmes kept his cool manner until our visitor had left us, although it was easy for me, who knew him so well, to see that he was just waiting to get to work on the problem. The moment that broad back had gone through the door, my friend rushed to the table, laid out all the pieces of paper containing dancing men in front of him, and threw himself into making sense of them. For two hours I watched him as he covered side after side of paper with figures and letters. So taken with his work was he, that he had completely forgotten that I was there. Finally he jumped from his chair with a cry of pleasure, and walked up and down the room looking pleased with himself. Then he wrote a long telegram. "If my answer to this is as I hope, you will have a very pretty case to add to your notebook, Watson," said he. "I expect that we shall be able to go down to Norfolk tomorrow, and to take our friend some news as to what it all means."

I must say that I wanted to know what he had found out, but I knew that Holmes liked to tell things at his own time and in his own way, so I waited until it should suit him to tell me about it.

But the answering telegram did not come for two days, during which time Holmes started at every ring of the bell. On the second evening there came a letter from Hilton Cubitt. A set of dancing men had appeared that morning upon the sunclock. He enclosed a copy of it, which is here reproduced:

■cool manner 冷静な態度 ■get to work 仕事に取り掛かる ■lay out 適切に［きちんと］並べる ■contain 動 含む ■throw oneself into （仕事などに）打ち込む ■side after side of paper 次々と紙に ■enclose 動 〜を同封する ■reproduced 動 〜を再現する

シャーロック・ホームズは、客が立ち去るまで冷静さを保っていたが、彼を
よく知る私には、彼がすぐに仕事にかかりたくてうずうずしていることが見て
とれた。客の広い背中がドアの向こうに消えたとたんに机に向かい、踊る人形
が描かれた紙きれを残らず並べ、解読にかかった。2時間の間、私は紙に次々
と数字と文字を書きつけるホームズの姿を見ていた。仕事に没頭しすぎて、私
がいることなどすっかり忘れているようであった。最後には喜びの声をあげて
椅子から跳び上がり、嬉しくてたまらない様子で部屋の中を歩き回った。それ
から長い電報を書いた。「僕が出した答えが正解だとすると、君の事件簿に、
また新たな愛すべき事件を加えることができるよ、ワトソン君。明日、ノー
フォークに行って、友人に、この事件の意味するところについて、何かしら新
しいことを知らせることができるだろう」

　私はホームズが発見した内容を知りたかった。でも、彼は自分のタイミング
と自分の流儀で物事を話したいのだということもわかっていた。だから、彼に
とって私に話す時期が来るまで待たなくてはならない。
　だが、電報の返事は2日待ってもこなかった。ホームズは呼び鈴にずっと注
意していた。2日目の夕方、ヒルトン・キュービットから一通の手紙が届いた。
その日の朝、日時計の上に踊る人形たちが描かれていたようで、その写しが同
封されていた。この絵である。

ᚷᚪᚾᚳᚣᚳᛂ ᚠᚷᚻᚴᚠᚷ
ᚷᚷᚷᛂᛂᛂᚣᛁᚴᚣᛁᚷ

Holmes looked at this new statement for some minutes, and then suddenly jumped to his feet with a cry of surprise. His face was white with fear.

"We have let this case go far enough," said he. "Is there a train to North Walsham tonight?"

I looked in the timetable; the last had just gone.

"Then we shall breakfast early and take the very first in the morning," said Holmes. "We must get there as soon as possible. Ah! Here is the telegram I have been waiting for." He tore it open. "This makes it even more necessary that we should not lose an hour in letting Hilton Cubitt know how things stand, for it is a dangerous position in which our simple Norfolk farmer finds himself."

So, indeed, it proved, and we come to the unhappy ending of a story which had seemed at the start to hold no danger. I would like to give some good news, but I must tell my readers the facts that made Riding Thorpe Manor famous throughout England.

■statement 图 声明　■white with fear 恐怖で青ざめる　■go far enough 十分引き伸ばす　■timetable 图 時刻表　■tear ~ open ~を破いて開ける　■how things stand どういう状況か　■come to（良くない状態に）終わる　■at the start 最初に、初めは　■hold no danger 何の危険もはらまない

　ホームズは数分の間、この新しい絵を見ていたが、突然、驚きの声をあげて立ちあがった。顔が恐怖で真っ青になっている。

　「これ以上は引き延ばせない。今夜、ノース・ウォルシャム行きの列車はあるかな?」
　私は時刻表を調べた。最終電車が出たところだった。
　「それでは朝食を早めにとって、朝一番の列車に乗ろう。できるだけ早く向かわなくては。おお!　待っていた電報だ」と開封する。「一時間だって無駄にはできない。ヒルトン・キュービット氏に事の次第を知らせなければ。あの実直なノーフォークの地主は、今とても危険な状況にいるんだ」

　実際、その通りだった。最初は何の危険もないように思えたこのストーリーは不幸な結末を迎えた。読者の皆さんにはよい知らせを届けられればよかったのだが、リドリング・ソープ荘園の名前がイギリス中で話題に上ることになったという事実を伝えなくてはならない。

We had hardly alighted at North Walsham, when the stationmaster hurried towards us. "I suppose you are the detectives from London?" said he.

A look of fear passed over Holmes's face.

"What makes you think such a thing?"

"Because Inspector Martin from Norwich has just passed through. But maybe you are the doctors. She's not dead—or wasn't the last I heard. You may be in time to save her yet, though it be for the hangman."

Holmes's face darkened.

"We are going to Riding Thorpe Manor, but have heard nothing of what has passed there."

"It's a bad business," said the stationmaster. "They are shot, both Mr. Hilton Cubitt and his wife. She shot him, and then herself, so the servants say. He's dead and it's expected she will follow him. Dear, dear, one of the oldest families in Norfolk, and one of the most liked."

Without a word Holmes hurried to a cab, and during the long drive he did not open his mouth. Never have I seen him so upset. He had been uneasy during the journey from town, and I had noticed that he had looked nervously in the morning newspapers. But now this sudden realization of his worst fears left him in a deep sadness. He sat back in his seat, lost in his unhappy thoughts. Yet there was much around to interest us, for we were passing through

■alight 動 (乗物から)降りる　■stationmaster 名 駅長　■pass over 横切る　■inspector 名 警部　■in time 間に合って　■hangman 名 絞首刑執行人　■darken 動 暗くなる　■bad business ひどいこと、困ったこと

　ノース・ウォルシャムで下車すると、駅長が駆け寄ってきた。「ロンドンからいらした探偵さんですね？」

　ホームズの顔に不安が走った。
「なぜそう思われるのですか？」
「先程マーティン警部がノリッジからいらしたのです。いや、もしかしたらお医者様でいらっしゃいますか。奥さんはまだ息がある。私が最後に聞いたところでは。まだ間に合うかもしれません。でも、いずれ絞首刑になるでしょうが」
　ホームズの顔がかげった。
「リドリング・ソープ荘園に行こうと思っているのですが、そこで何が起こったのか何も聞いていないのです」
「ひどい事件です」と駅長が言った。「ヒルトン・キュービット氏と奥さんが撃たれたのです。奥さんがヒルトン氏を撃ち、それから自分を撃ったと使用人は言っています。氏は亡くなりました。奥さんもおそらくだめでしょう。ああ、ノーフォーク一の旧家で、皆に愛されていたのに」

　ホームズは無言で馬車へ駆け込み、長い道中、一言も口を開かなかった。彼がここまでショックを受けているのを見たことがない。道中ずっと、ぴりぴりし通しだった。私はホームズを眺めていた。彼は朝刊を不安そうに眺めていたが、最悪の予想が現実になったとわかった瞬間、深い悲しみに襲われ、座席にもたれ絶望に沈みこんだ。しかし、私たちの周りには興味をひく光景が広がっていた。というのは、馬車はイングランドのなかでも有数の田園地域を走って

one of the most unusual parts of England. A few houses, each one far apart from the next, represented the people who lived there now, while on every side great, square churches reached to the sky from the flat green land and told of the pride and richness of old East Anglia. At last we saw the German Ocean over the green edge of Norfolk, and the driver pointed to an old house set in a wood. "That's Riding Thorpe Manor," said he.

As we drove up to the front door, I saw in front of it, beside the grass, the clock and stables which the late Hilton Cubitt had told us about. A little man with a quick, bright manner had just arrived himself. He told us he was Inspector Martin, of the Norfolk police force, and he was very surprised when he heard the name of my companion.

"Why, Mr. Holmes, the crime only happened at three this morning. How could you hear of it in London and get down here as soon as I?"

"I felt something would happen. I came in the hope of stopping it."

"Then you must have some important evidence that we don't know about for they were said to be a most happy couple."

■represent 動 表す、示す ■flat 形 平坦な ■pride 形 全盛(期) ■richness 形 豊かさ
■East Anglia 東アングリア《イギリス東部の半島で、古代の東アングリア王国があった》
■German Ocean ゲルマン海《現在の北海》 ■get down (乗り物などから)降りる ■in
the hope of ～を望んで

いたのだ。ぽつりぽつりと家が見え、この地に住む人の数を物語る。一方で、両側には、広々とした緑の土地に四角い塔の巨大な教会がいくつかそびえ立ち、旧東アングリア王国の栄華を物語っている。やがて、ノーフォークの緑の海岸線の向こう側にゲルマン海（北海の別名）が見えてきた。御者は森の中に建つ古風な家を指さして言った。「あれがリドリング・ソープ荘園です」

正面玄関に着くと、屋敷の正面脇に、在りし日のヒルトン氏が説明してくれた芝生と日時計、納屋があった。きびきびとした動作の小柄な男がちょうど到着したところだった。彼は私たちに、ノーフォーク警察のマーティン警部だと名乗った。彼は私の連れの名前を聞いて、とても驚いた。

「ホームズさん、事件は今朝3時に起こったのですよ。いったいどうやってロンドンから聞きつけて、私と同時にこちらに着くなんてことができたのでしょうか」

「何か起こるのではと感じたのです。防げればいいがと思ってやって来ました」

「それでは、重要な証拠をおもちなのでしょうね。どうもわからないのです。このご夫婦は仲がよかったという評判ですから」

"I have only the evidence of the dancing men," said Holmes. "I will explain the matter to you later. Meanwhile, as it is too late to save Mr. Hilton Cubitt, I want to make sure that I use what I know to make sure the truth is known. Should I help you in your investigation, or would you like me to work alone?"

"I should be proud to think that we were acting together, Mr. Holmes," said the policeman.

"In that case I should be glad to hear the evidence and to take a look at the house as soon as possible."

Inspector Martin had the good sense to allow my friend to do things in his own manner, and he just carefully noted the results. The doctor, an old, white-haired man, had just come down from Mrs. Cubitt's room, and he reported that her wounds were grave, but he thought that she would live. The bullet had passed through the front of her head and it would probably be some time before she would come round. On the question of whether she had been shot or had shot herself, he would not give an opinion. The bullet had been fired at very close quarters. There was only one gun found in the room, from which two bullets had been fired. Mr. Hilton Cubitt had been shot through the heart. It was equally possible that he had shot her then himself, or that she had been the criminal, for the gun lay upon the floor halfway between them.

■in that case もしそうなら　■take a look at ～をちょっと見る　■have the good sense to ～する分別 [良識] がある　■pass through 貫通する　■some time いつか ■come round 意識を回復する　■on the question of ～の問題について　■at close quarters 間近に、接近して　■shot through the heart 心臓を撃ち抜かれて　■lie upon the floor 床の上に落ちている　■halfway between ～の真ん中に

226

「証拠といっても、踊る人形の絵だけです。あとでご説明しましょう。ヒルトン・キュービット氏を救うのには間に合わなかったけれど、私が持っている情報を活用して、真実が解明されることを望んでいます。捜査をお手伝いした方がいいですか？　それとも私は単独で進めたほうがよろしいでしょうか?」

「ご一緒させていただければ光栄です、ホームズさん」と警部は言った。

「そうしていただけるなら、すぐにでも聞きとりと現場検証にかかりたいのですが」

　マーティン警部はよくできた人物で、わが友人が自分のやり方ですすめることに嫌な顔をせず、ただその結果を丁寧にメモしていた。白髪の医者がキュービット夫人の部屋から降りてきて、傷は深いが命に別状はないだろうと報告した。弾丸が前頭部を打ち抜いているので、意識を取り戻すにはしばらく時間がかかるだろうとのことだった。誰かに撃たれたのか、それとも自分で撃ったのかということについては、医師は自分の意見を述べることはしなかった。弾丸はごく近い位置から発射されていた。室内には拳銃が一丁だけあり、その拳銃から2発の弾丸が発射されていた。ヒルトン・キュービット氏は心臓を撃ち抜かれていた。拳銃が二人の間に落ちていたので、氏が夫人を撃ってから自分を撃ったとも、夫人が犯人だとも、どちらの可能性もあった。

"Has he been moved?" asked Holmes.

"We have moved nothing except the lady. We could not leave her lying wounded on the floor."

"How long have you been here, Doctor?"

"Since four o'clock."

"Anyone else?"

"Yes, the policeman here."

"And you have touched nothing?"

"Nothing."

"You have acted with great sense. Who sent for you?"

"The house servant."

"Was it she who called the police?"

"She and Mrs. King, the cook."

"Where are they now?"

"In the kitchen, I believe."

"Then I think we had better hear their story at once."

The old hall had been turned into an office for the police. Holmes sat in a great old chair, his eyes looking all around. I could read in them a set purpose to find out the true story of what had happened at Riding Thorpe Manor, and to clear the family name of Hilton Cubitt. Inspector Martin, the country doctor, myself, and a large policeman made up the rest of that strange company.

■with great sense 素晴らしい判断で　■send for ～を呼び寄せる　■house servant 家政婦　■had better ～した方がよい　■set purpose はっきりした目的　■make up 成り立っている　■company 名 同席の人、一団

228

「遺体は移動させていないですね?」とホームズは尋ねた。

「奥さん以外は何も動かしていません。傷を負ったまま床の上に放っておくわけにはいきませんから」

「先生はいつからこちらに?」

「4時からおります」

「ほかに誰かいましたか」

「はい、そこにいる警察の方が」

「何も触れていませんか?」

「ええ、何も」

「よく心得ておいででしたね。誰に呼ばれたのですか?」

「この家の使用人の女性です」

「その人が警察を呼んだのでしょうか」

「ええ、彼女と料理人のキングさんが」

「ふたりは今どこにいますか?」

「台所でしょう」

「では、さっそくおふたりの話をうかがったほうがいいでしょうね」

古い広間が事情聴取の場所となった。ホームズは古風な大椅子に腰を下ろし、あたりにくまなく目を光らせた。私はその目に、リドリング・ソープ荘園で起こった事件の真相を明らかにし、キュービット家の潔白を証明するのだという決意が見てとれた。ホームズの他に、マーティン警部と地元の医師、私、大柄の警察官という妙なメンバーで聴取が始まった。

The two women told their story clearly enough. They had been awakened from their sleep by a loud noise, which had been followed a minute later by a second one. They rushed out of their rooms and together they had gone downstairs. The door of the study was open and a candle was burning upon the table. Their master lay upon his face in the middle of the room. He was dead. Near the window his wife was lying, her head against the wall. She was badly wounded, and the side of her face was red with blood. She was clearly alive, but was unable to speak. The hall, as well as the room, was full of smoke and the smell of powder. The window was closed and fastened on the inside. Both women were sure about that. They had at once sent for the doctor and the police. Then, with the help of the stable-boy, they had carried the wounded lady to her room. Both she and her husband had been to bed, and they were both still wearing their night-clothes. Nothing had been moved in the study. So far as they knew, there had never been any problem between husband and wife. They had always looked upon them as a very happy couple.

■awaken 動 目覚める　■rush out of one's room　～の部屋から飛び出す
■downstairs 副 階下に　■candle 名 ろうそく　■master 名 主人　■lie upon one's
face うつ伏せに横たわる　■powder 名 火薬　■fasten 動 ～を（ピタリと）閉める

　ふたりの女性はわかりやすく話してくれた。大きな音がして目が覚め、1分ほどしてもう一発の音が聞こえた。ふたりは部屋から走り出て、一緒に階段を下りた。書斎の扉が開いていて、テーブルの上にろうそくが灯っていた。家の主が部屋の真ん中にうつぶせに倒れていた。息はなかった。窓のそばには夫人が、壁に頭をもたせかけて横たわっていた。重傷で、顔の側面が血で真っ赤に染まっていた。息があるのはたしかだったが、話をするのは無理だった。室内はもちろん、廊下にも硝煙と火薬の匂いが充満していた。窓は締まっていて、内側から鍵がかかっていた、ふたりとも、この点については間違いないと言った。ふたりはすぐに医者と警官を呼び、馬番の少年に手伝わせ、負傷した夫人を自室に移した。夫人も氏も、寝間着を着ており、事件が起こる前に床についていた形跡があった。書斎の中は、何も動かされていなかった。ふたりの知る限りでは、夫婦のあいだに諍いがあったことはなく、いつも幸せそうにしか見えなかった。

■on the inside 内側から　■be sure about ～に確信を持っている　■had been to bed 床についていた　■night-clothes 名 寝間着　■so far as ～に関する限り　■look upon ～ as ～を…と見なす

These were the facts of the servants' evidence. In answer to Inspector Martin, they were clear that every door was fastened upon the inside, and that no one could have escaped from the house. In answer to Holmes, they both said they were sure that they could smell powder from the moment that they ran out of their rooms on the top floor. "That is a very important point," said Holmes to Inspector Martin. "And now I think we are in a position to undertake a careful investigation of the room."

The study proved to be a small room, lined on three sides with books, and with a writing table facing a window, which looked out upon the garden. We first looked at the body of Hilton Cubitt which lay stretched across the room. The state of his clothes showed that he had come straight from his bedroom. The bullet had been fired at him from the front, hitting his heart. There was no mark on his back, so the bullet had stayed in his body. His death had been quick and painless. There was no powder-marking either upon his clothes or on his hands. According to the country doctor, the lady had powder marks on her face but not on her hands.

■in answer to ～に対する答弁として　■top floor 最上階　■undertake ～に取り掛かる　■proved to be ～だと分かる　■line 動 並ぶ　■writing table 書き物机　■face 動 ～の方を向く　■look out upon ～に面する　■body 名 遺体　■lie stretched across

　これがふたりの証言から得た情報である。マーティン警部の質問に対して、どの扉も内側から鍵がかけられていたことは確かで、家から逃げた人物もいないと答えた。ホームズの質問に対しては、一番上の階にある自分たちの部屋から飛び出してきたときには、たしかに火薬の匂いがしていたと答えた。「これはとても重要なことです」とホームズは警部に言った。「今度は、部屋を徹底的に調べてみましょう」

　書斎は小さな部屋で、三方に本棚があり、窓に面して書き物机が置かれ、そこから庭を見渡すことができた。私たちはまず、部屋を横切るように横たわっているヒルトン・キュービット氏の遺体を調べた。着衣の状況からみて、寝室からまっすぐにここへ来たのだろうと思われた。弾丸は正面から発射され、心臓に届いていた。背中に傷跡がないところをみると、体内にとどまっているようだ。即死で苦しむ間もなかっただろう。衣服と両手のどちらにも火薬の跡はない。医師によると、夫人は顔にその跡があったが、手にはなかったとのことだ。

〜を分割するように横たわる　■come straight from　〜からまっすぐにやってくる　■hit 動 〜に命中させる　■painless 形 痛みを伴わない　■powder-marking 名 火薬の痕跡　■according to 〜によれば

"Having no powder marks means nothing, though having them may mean everything," said Holmes. "Unless the powder from a badly fitting bullet happens to fly backward, one may fire many shots without leaving a sign. I would say that Mr. Cubitt's body may now be removed. I suppose, Doctor, you have not recovered the bullet which wounded the lady?"

"We cannot do that until she recovers a little. But there are still four bullets in the gun. Two have been fired and two wounds made, so that each bullet can be accounted for."

"So it would seem," said Holmes. "Perhaps you can account also for the bullet which has so clearly hit the edge of the window?"

He had turned suddenly, and his long, thin finger was pointing to a hole which had been made just below the lower window.

"By Heaven!" cried Inspector Martin. "How ever did you see that?"

"Because I looked for it."

"Wonderful!" said the country doctor. "You are right, sir. Then a third shot has been fired, and therefore a third person must have been present. But who could that have been, and how could he have got away?"

"That is the question which we are now about to answer," said Sherlock Holmes.

■badly fitting bullet うまく装填されていない銃弾　■happen to 偶然〜する ■backward 副 後方へ、逆に　■leave a sign 痕跡を残す　■recover 動 回復する　■can be accounted for 勘定が合う、説明がつく　■so clearly 明らかに　■By Heaven! 「神に誓って」

「火薬の跡がないということからは何もわかりませんね。あれば全てわかりそうなんですが」とホームズは言った。「弾の込め方が悪くて火薬が後ろへ飛ぶようなことがない限り、痕跡を残さずに何発も撃つことができます。キュービット氏の遺体はもう動かしていいでしょう。先生、夫人を撃った弾丸はまだ摘出していませんよね」

「もう少し回復なさるまで無理です。でも、銃にはまだ4発残っています。2発が発射されて2人が負傷したので、勘定は合っています」

「まぁ、そう見えますね。でも、あの窓の縁に撃ち込まれた弾丸も勘定に入れたほうがいいですよ」とホームズが言った。

そしてひょいと振り返ると、長くてほっそりした指で、下の窓枠の底のすぐ下にできている穴を指さした。

「本当だ!」とマーティン警部が叫んだ。「どうやってこれを見つけたのですか?」

「探していたからです」

「なんていうことだ! あなたのおっしゃる通りです。3発目が撃たれたということは、3人目の人物がいるということになりますね。でも、誰がここにいたのでしょう、それにどうやって逃げたのでしょうか?」

「それこそが、今私たちが取り組んでいる問題です」とホームズが答えた。

"You remember, Inspector Martin, when the servants said that on leaving their room they noticed at once a smell of powder, I said that the point was a very important one?"

"Yes, Mr. Holmes, but I must say I did not quite follow you."

"It seemed to point to the fact that at the time of the firing, the window as well as the door of the room had been open. Otherwise the smell of powder could not have been blown so quickly through the house. A through wind in the room was necessary for that. Both door and window were only open for a short time, however."

"How do you prove that?"

"Because the candle had burned evenly on all sides."

"Wonderful!" cried Inspector Martin. "Wonderful!"

"Feeling sure that the window had been open at the time of the shots, I thought that there might have been a third person, who stood outside this opening and fired through it. Any shot directed at this person might hit the sill. I looked, and there, sure enough, was the bullet mark!"

"But how came the window to be shut and fastened?"

"The woman's first thought would be to shut and fasten the window. But, look, what is this?"

■on leaving one's room 部屋を出るや否や　■follow 動 話について行く、理解する　■point to the fact that ～という事実を指摘する　■firing 名 発砲　■otherwise 副 さもなければ　■blow 動（物が風に）吹かれる　■through wind 形 通り抜ける風　■evenly 副 均一に、均等に　■feel sure 確かだと感じる　■direct at ～に向ける　■sill 名 窓の下枠　■sure enough 思った通り、案の定　■bullet mark 弾痕

236

「マーティン警部、使用人の女性たちが部屋を出てすぐに火薬の匂いがした
と行った時、私はこの点が大変重要だと言いましたよね。憶えていますか?」

「もちろんです、ホームズさん。でも、実はどういうことかわっていませ
んでした」

「それはね、発砲されたときに、窓も部屋の扉も開いていたということを意
味するのです。そうでないと、そんな短時間に煙が家じゅうにたちこめるわけ
がない。部屋を吹き抜ける風がなくてはね。でも、ドアと窓の両方が開いて
たのはごくわずかの時間です」

「なぜそう言い切れるのですか?」

「ろうそくの蝋が偏りなく均等に流れています」

「素晴らしい。素晴らしいです!」と警部が叫んだ。

「銃が撃たれたときに窓が開いていたのが確かなら、3番目の人物がいた。そ
の人物は開いていた窓の外から発砲したのです。そしてその人物に向けて撃た
れた弾丸が窓の枠に当たったかもしれない。よくみると、たしかに弾の痕があ
りました」

「しかし、窓が閉められ、掛け金がかかっていたのはなぜでしょう?」

「奥さんがとっさに窓を閉めて掛け金をおろしたのでしょうね。しかし見て
下さい、これは何でしょうか」

It was a lady's handbag which stood upon the study table. Holmes opened it and emptied it onto the table. There were twenty fifty-pound notes—and nothing else.

"This must be kept, for it is very likely to be evidence," said Holmes, as he handed the bag and money to Inspector Martin. "It is now necessary that we should try to throw some light upon this third bullet, which has clearly, from the marking of the wood, been fired from inside the room. I should like to see Mrs. King again. You said, Mrs. King, that you were awakened by a loud noise—what we now know to be a gun going off. When you said that, did you mean that it seemed to you to be louder than the second one?"

"Well, sir, it wakened me from my sleep, so it is hard to judge. But it did seem very loud."

"You don't think that it might have been two shots fired almost at the same moment?"

"I am sure I couldn't say, sir."

"I believe that it was undoubtedly so. I rather think, Inspector Martin, that we have now learned all that this room can teach us. If you will kindly step round with me, we shall see what fresh evidence the garden has to offer."

■empty 動（中身を）出す（容器などを）空にする　■note 名 紙幣　■throw light upon ～を解明する　■go off 発射する　■judge 動 判断する　■undoubtedly 副 疑いようもなく　■kindly 副 どうか～　■step round 歩きまわる

　書斎の机の上に女性もののハンドバッグがあった。ホームズが開けて中のものを机の上に出した。25ポンド紙幣の束、それだけだった。

　「保管しておきましょう。証拠として必要になりそうです」。ホームズはバッグと紙幣を警部に渡しながら言った。「マーティン警部、次はこの3番目の弾丸について考えてみましょうか。窓木に残った跡から見て、室内から発砲したのは間違いないでしょう。料理人のキング夫人にお聞きしなくては。キングさん、あなたは大きな音、つまり銃の発射音だったわけですが、その音で目が覚めたと言っていましたね。そうおっしゃるということは、2発目の音よりも最初の音の方が大きかったということですか?」

　「そうですね、最初の音で目が覚めたので、なんとも言いかねます。でもとても大きな音でした」
　「二発がほぼ同時に撃たれたとは考えられませんか」

　「わかりません」
　「僕はそうに違いないとにらんでいるんですがね。マーティン警部、もうこの部屋から得られる情報はないと思います。よろしければ庭を回って、新しい証拠を探しませんか」

A flowerbed ran up to the study window. All of us except Holmes were surprised to see that the flowers had been stepped on, and the soft soil had many footmarks. Holmes hunted about among the grass and flowers like a dog after a wounded bird. Then, with a cry of pleasure, he picked up a little bullet-case.

"I thought so," said he; "here is the third bullet-case. I really think, Inspector Martin, that our case is almost complete."

The country policeman's face had shown his complete surprise at the fast and masterful way Holmes had run his investigation. At first he had shown some signs of wanting to do things his way, but now he was overcome by Holmes's methods and was ready to follow, without question, wherever Holmes led.

"Who do you think did it?" he asked.

"I'll go into that later. There are several points in this problem that I have not been able to explain to you yet. Now that I have got so far, I had best carry on along my own lines, and then clear the matter up once and for all."

"Just as you wish, Mr. Holmes, so long as we get our man."

"I do not mean to be difficult, but it is not possible, at the moment of action, to enter into long explanations. I now know almost everything about this case. Even if this lady should never recover, we can still work out the events of last night, and ensure that the criminal is caught. First of all, I wish to know if there is any place in this area known as Elrige's?"

■flowerbed 图 花壇　■run up to ～に達する　■step on ～を踏みつける　■soft soil 柔らかい土　■footmark 图 足跡　■hunt about 探しまわる　■after 前 ～の後を追って　■pick up 拾い上げる　■bullet-case 图 薬莢　■masterful 形 優れた技量の　■overcome 動（相手を）圧倒する　■go into 詳しく述べる

書斎の窓の下から花壇が伸びている。花が踏みにじられ、柔らかな土にはたくさんの足跡がついていて、ホームズ以外の面々はあっと驚いた。ホームズは撃たれた鳥を探す猟犬のように草花の間を調べ回った。そして、喜びの声とともに、小さな薬莢（弾丸を入れておく筒）を拾いあげた。

「思った通りだ。これが3発目の薬莢です。マーティン警部、この事件もほぼ解決のようですね」

この田舎の警部の顔に、ホームズの迅速で巧みな捜査に感嘆する様子が見てとれた。最初のころは自分の流儀で進めたそうなそぶりを見せていたが、今ではもう、ホームズのやり方に対抗しようとはしなくなり、ホームズに言われるままに付いてきていた。

「犯人は誰だとお思いですか?」と警部が尋ねた。

「それについては後で。この問題にはまだいくつか説明できないことがあります。でも、ここまで来ましたから、この方針のまま続けていくのが一番だと思います。その後、一度にすべてを明らかにしたいのですが」

「ええ、おまかせいたしますよ、ホームズさん。犯人さえ逮捕できればいいのです」

「難しいと言う意味ではなくて、不可能なのですよ。行動中に長い説明をするというのがね。この事件の真相はほぼ解明いたしました。夫人の意識が戻らなかったとしても、昨夜の顛末を明らかにして犯人をつかまえることができます。まず、このあたりに『エルリッジ』という名前の場所があるかどうかを知りたいのですが」

■had best ～するのが一番よい　■carry on 続行する　■along one's own line 自分の方針に沿って　■once and for all きっぱりと、決定的に　■so long as ～さえすれば　■ensure 動 ～を確かにする　■wish to know if ～かどうか知りたい

The servants were questioned, but none of them had heard of such a place. The stable-boy, however, remembered that a farmer of that name lived some miles off, in the direction of East Rushton.

"Is it a lonely farm?"

"Very lonely, sir."

"Perhaps they have not heard yet of all that happened during the night?"

"Perhaps not, sir."

Holmes thought for a little, then a strange smile played over his face.

"Get a horse ready, my boy," said he, "I wish you to take a note to Elrige's Farm."

He took from his pocket the various pieces of paper that contained the dancing men. With these in front of him, he worked for some time at the study-table. At last he handed a note to the boy, with directions to put it into the hands of the person to whom it was addressed, and to answer no questions of any sort that might be put to him. I saw the outside of the note, written in strange, thin characters, very unlike Holmes's usual writing. It was to Mr. Abe Slaney, Elrige's Farm, East Rushton, Norfolk.

■mile 图 マイル《距離の単位、約1,609m》 ■for a little しばらくの間 ■smile played over ～に微笑が浮かぶ ■get ready 用意する ■various 形 個々の ■contain 動 含む ■with these in front of これらを～の前に置くと ■for some time しばらくの間 ■direction 图 指図 ■thin character 細い文字 ■very unlike 似ても似つかぬ

使用人たちに尋ねてみたが、誰も聞いたことがないと言う。しかし、馬番の少年から、数マイル先、イースト・ラストンの方角に、そういう名前の農場主がいるとの情報を引き出すことができた。

「辺ぴなところにあるのかな?」

「ええ、とても」

「それなら、そこにいる人たちはこの夜に起こったことを知らないだろうね」

「ええ、おそらく」

ホームズは少し考えてから、何とも不思議な微笑を浮かべた。

「君、馬の用意をしてくれ」と彼は言った。「そのエルリッジ農場へ、手紙を届けてほしいんだ」

ホームズはポケットから、踊る人形が描かれた種々の紙を取り出した。そして自分の前に広げると、しばらく書斎の机に向かった。やがて、一通の手紙を少年に渡し、この宛名の人物に直接渡すこと、どんな質問をされたとしても決して答えないこと、との指示を出した。私はその手紙の宛名を見たが、ホームズのいつもの筆跡とは似ても似つかぬ、ぎくしゃくとした不ぞろいの文字で、ノーフォーク州、イースト・ラストン、エルリッジ農場、エイブ・スレイニー様と書かれていた。

25

"I think, Inspector Martin," Holmes said, "that you would do well to send for help, as if it works out according to plan, you may have a dangerous man to guard. If there is an afternoon train to town, Watson, I think we should do well to take it, as this investigation draws quickly to a close."

When the young man had been sent with the note, Sherlock Holmes spoke again to the servants. If any visitor were to call asking for Mrs. Hilton Cubitt, nothing should be said as to her condition, but he was to be shown at once into the living room. Then he led the way into the living room, saying that the business was now out of our hands, and that we must while away the time as best we might until we could see what was in store for us. The doctor had already left, and only Inspector Martin and myself were still there.

"I think that I can help you pass an hour in an interesting way," said Holmes, pulling his chair up to the table, and placing out in front of him the various papers upon which were recorded the groups of dancing men. "As to you, friend Watson, I must say sorry for having kept you in the dark for so long. I think, Inspector Martin, that you as a policeman might be very interested in this case. I must tell you, first of all, how we came to be connected with Mr. Hilton Cubitt and this case." He then shortly retold the facts which have already been recorded. "I have here in front of me these unusual pictures, at which one might smile had they not

■would do well to ～したらよいだろう　■send for help ～を呼び寄せる　■work out うまくいく　■according to plan 計画通り　■draw to a close 終わりに近づく　■call 動 ちょっと訪問する　■as to ～に関しては　■show someone into （人）を～に案内する　■lead the way into 先頭に立って～の中へ行く

「警部、応援を要請した方がいいかと思います。僕の予測どおりに事が進む
とすれば、大変危険な男を保護することになります。ワトソン君、午後に街へ
向かう列車があれば、乗ったほうがいいだろうね。この捜査はもうすぐ終わ
る」

　少年が手紙を持って出発すると、シャーロック・ホームズは、再び使用人た
ちに向かって、ヒルトン・キュービット夫人を訪ねてくる者がいたとしても、
容態を知らせないようにし、その者をすぐに居間に通すこと、との指示を出し
た。それから彼は、仕事はもう自分たちの手を離れたから、次の展開までの
んびりしよう、と言いながら居間に向かった。医師はすでに屋敷を後にしてい
て、マーティン警部と私だけが残っていた。

　「では、これから1時間をおふたりが楽しくすごせるようにお手伝いしましょ
う」とホームズは言い、椅子を机の方へ引き寄せて、踊る人形たちを記録した
それぞれの紙切れを前に並べた。「ワトソン君、友人である君をこんなに長い
間、謎解きをせぬままに待たせてしまったことを謝らなくてはならないね。そ
れから警部、あなたも当然、この事件に強い関心をおもちのことでしょう。ま
ずは、私たちがヒルトン氏、そしてこの事件と関わったいきさつをお話ししま
しょう」。そしてホームズは、私がここまで記してきた内容を簡潔に説明した。
「私の前に、奇妙な絵が並んでいます。このような不幸な結末につながったも

■out of one's hands（仕事が）（人）の手を離れて　■while away のんびりと過ごす
■in store for ～に備えて　■up to ～まで　■place out 広げて置く　■keep ～ in the
dark ～を秘密にしておく　■retold 動 retell（～を再び語る）の過去形

led to such an unhappy ending. I know a lot about all forms of secret writings, and am myself the writer of a small and not very good article upon the subject, in which I analyze many of them, but I must say that this one was new to me. The object of those that thought up the system was to hide that these characters mean something, and to give the idea that they are only pictures done by children.

"Having once realized, however, that the characters stood for letters, and having used the rules which guide us in all forms of secret writings, the answer was easy enough. The first message given to me was so short that all I could safely say was that the character 𝍨 stood for E. As you know, E is the most used letter in the English language, and is used so much more than any other single letter that even in a short passage one would expect to find it most often. Out of fifteen characters in the first group, four were the same, so it was reasonable to set this down as E. It is true that in some cases the figure was holding a flag, and in some cases not, but it was probable, from the way in which the flags were used that they showed the end of a word. I therefore noted that E was represented by 𝍨.

■secret writings 暗号記号　■article 图 記事　■analyze 動 分析する　■think up 考え出す　■stand for ～を表す　■letter 图 文字　■rule 图 規則　■safely 副 支障なく　■as you know ご承知の通り　■passage 图 一節、一句　■set down ～ as ～を…であるとみなす　■flag 图 旗　■probable 形 確からしい　■word 图 単語　■be represented by ～で表される

のでなければ、他愛ない代物です。私はさまざまな暗号の形式について造詣がありまして、このテーマで細やかな記事も書いたことがあります。その中では多くの暗号を分析したのですが、実はこのようなものは見たことがありませんでした。この暗号の規則を考えた人間の目的は、この絵が何かしらの意味をもつということを隠し、子どもの落書きにすぎないという印象を与えることでしょう」

「人形の記号が文字に対応していると見抜いて、あとはあらゆる型の暗号に通じる規則をあてはめていくと、簡単に解読できるのです。最初のメッセージは短すぎて、間違いなく言えたのは、この人形 が アルファベットのEであることだけです。ご存じのように、Eは英語では最も頻繁に使われる文字で、その使用頻度は他のどの文字よりも高く、短い文の中でも一番たくさん使われます。最初のメッセージにある15個の絵のうち4つが同じものでした。それならば、この絵をEとするのが妥当でしょう。旗をもっている場合ともっていない場合があるのですが、その使われ方からみると、旗は単語の区切りの印を意味するのではなないかと考えました。それで、Eはこの絵 で表されるのだと考えました。

"But now came the real difficulty of the investigation. The order of the English letters after E is by no means well marked. Speaking generally, T, A, O, I, N, S, H, R, D, and L are the order in which letters are most used; but T, A, O, and I are all used about the same, and it would be an endless job to try each possible set of letters until a meaning was arrived at. I therefore waited for fresh material. In my second meeting with Mr. Hilton Cubitt, he was able to give me three other short groups, one of which appeared—as there were no flags—to be a single word. Here are the characters. Now in the single word I have already got the two E's coming second and fourth in a word of five letters. It came to me that 'never' in reply to a question was quite likely. The position of this group on the stable door made me think that it was a reply written by the lady. Accepting this as right we are now able to say the characters ⚘⚘⚘ stand for N, V, and R.

■investigation 图 調査、研究　■order 图 順序　■by no means 決して～ではない
■well marked はっきり識別できる、明確な　■generally 副 通常　■endless 形 いつ終わるともしれない　■arrive at ～に達する　■material 图 材料　■appear 動 ～と思われる　■come to 思い付く　■in reply to ～への返答として　■quite likely 本当にありそうに　■accept ～ as ～を…と受け入れる

248

　しかし、ここからが暗号解読の本当に難しいところです。英語でEの次に頻繁に使われる英語の文字が何かということについては、決定的なものはありません。一般的には、頻度が高い順にT、A、O、I、N、S、H、R、D、Lと言われていますが、T、A、OとIはほとんど同じぐらいの頻度で登場しますから、意味のある文字の組み合わせを洗い出していたら、果てしない作業になります。それで私は、新たなデータを待ちました。ヒルトン氏は2度目の面談のときに、3つの短いサンプルを持ってきてくれました。そのうちのひとつは、旗が見あたらないので、1語だけだと思われました。これがその人形の並びです。5文字からなる1語のなかで、2番目と4番目にEが来るということがわかりました。そして、そのような単語の中で「never」（絶対にだめ）ならば、何かの呼びかけの応えとしてありえそうに思えました。納屋の扉に描かれていたときの状況から考えると、夫人が描いた返事ではないかと思いました。これが正しいとすると、この記号 はそれぞれ、N、V、Rということになります」

"Even now I was in considerable difficulty, but a happy thought enabled me to find several other letters. It seemed to me that if these words came, as I expected, from someone who had known the lady in her early life, a word which contained two E's with three letters in between might very well stand for the name 'ELSIE.' Looking at the groups I found that this word formed the end of the set which had been written three times. She was clearly being asked something. Now I had my L, S, and I. But what was she being asked? There were only four letters in the word in front of 'Elsie,' and it ended in E. Surely the word must be 'COME.' I tried all other four letters ending in E, but could find none to fit the case. So now I knew C, O, and M, and I was in a position to try the first group once more, dividing it into words and putting dots for characters which were still unknown. It came out in this way:

. M . ERE . . E SL . NE .

"Now the first letter can only be A, which is most useful, since it comes up no fewer than three times in this short passage, and it must be an H in the second word. Now it becomes:

AM HERE A . E SLANE .

■even now この期に及んで　■considerable 形 相当な　■difficulty 名 困難　■in between 間に　■surely 副 疑いなく　■divide 動 ～に分かれる　■come out ～という結果になる

　「これでもまだ先は長いと思われましたが、いくつかの文字について、あることがひらめいたのです。私が予測した通り、これが夫人の昔の知り合いからの暗号だとすれば、最初と最後がE、その中に3文字が挟まれている言葉は、夫人の名前「ELSIE」（エルシー）ではないだろうか。あらためて見てみると、3回の通信の末尾がこの組み合わせになっていました。これは夫人あての伝言とみて間違いなさそうです。こうしてL、S、Iがわかりました。でも、何を呼びかけていたのか。ELSIEの前には、たった4文字しかない単語が描かれているだけで、Eで終わっています。これは「COME」（来い）に間違いないでしょう。末尾がEで4文字の言葉をあれこれ調べてみましたが、どうもこの状況には合わないのです。そうしてC、O、Mが判明したので、もう一度最初のメッセージを見てみました。単語に区切り、まだ判明していない文字を点に置き換えてみると、このようになりました。

.M.ERE..E SL.NE.

　最初の文字は、この短い文章の中で3度も出てきます。これはAしかない。これは大変有益な発見でした。2つめの言葉にはHが入るに違いない。そうすれば、

AM HERE A.E SLANE.

Filling in the name:

AM HERE ABE SLANEY.

I had so many letters now that I could carry on with few problems to the second passage, which worked out in this fashion:

A . ELRI . ES

Here I could only make sense by putting T and G for the missing letters, and supposing that the name was that of some house or farm at which the writer was staying."

Inspector Martin and I had listened with interest to the full and clear account of how my friend had produced the results which had led to so complete an understanding of our difficulties.

"What did you do then, Mr. Holmes?" asked the policeman.

"I had every reason to suppose that this Abe Slaney was an American, since Abe is an American name, and since a letter from America had been the starting point of all the trouble. I had also cause to think, because of what the lady had said of her past, that there was some criminal secret in the matter. I therefore sent a telegram to my friend Wilson Hargreave, of the New York Police Office, who has more than once made use of my understanding of London crime. I asked him whether the name of Abe Slaney was

■carry on with ～を続ける　■in this fashion このように　■make sense 意味をなす
■account 图 説明　■produce 勔 作り出す　■result 图 結果　■since 瘘 ～なので
■have cause to ～する理由がある　■make use of ～を活用する

名前を入れれば

AM HERE ABE SLANEY.

（来たぞ、エイブ・スレイニー）

となります。

かなりの文字がわかったので、2番目の文章解析はそれほど問題なく進めることができました。このようになります。

A．ELRI．ES

ここでわかっていないところにＴとＧを入れると、何とか意味が通じる言葉になります。おそらく書き手が滞在しているエルリッジという家か農場の名前でしょう」

マーティン警部と私は、この完璧でわかりやすい説明に夢中で耳を傾けた。我が友が披露している結論は、目の前にある難事件を完全解決に導いていくものであった。

「ホームズさん、それからどうされたのですか」と警部が尋ねた。

「Abe Slaney（エイブ・スレイニー）なる人物は、どう見てもアメリカ人でしょうね、Abeはアメリカの名前ですし、アメリカから来た手紙がこの事件の発端だったのですから。また、自分の過去に対する夫人の話しぶりからみて、この事件には隠れた犯罪が絡んでいると考えられます。そこで私は、ニューヨーク警察にいる友人のウィルスン・ハーグリーヴへ電報を打ちました。ロンドンの事件ではたびたび協力した間柄です。彼に、エイブ・スレイニーという名前

known to him. Here is his reply: 'The most dangerous criminal in Chicago.' On the very evening upon which I had his answer, Hilton Cubitt sent me the last group of figures from Slaney. Working with known letters, it took this form:

ELSIE . RE . ARE TO MEET THY GO .

Adding two P's and a D completed a message that the man had moved on from asking Elsie to meet him to something much more dangerous. I at once came to Norfolk with Dr. Watson, but, unhappily, too late to stop what had happened."

"I am proud to have worked with you on this case," said Inspector Martin, warmly, "but I feel I must now say something. You are answerable only to yourself, but I am not. If this Abe Slaney, staying at Elrige's, is indeed the murderer, and if he has made his escape while I am seated here, I will get into grave trouble."

"You need not be uneasy. He will not try to escape."

"How do you know?"

"If he tried to run, it would tell everyone that he was the criminal."

"Then let us go to arrest him."

"I expect him here any moment."

■very evening まさに今夜　■move on 移る　■be proud to ～できて光栄だ
■answerable 形 釈明義務を負う　■to oneself 自分だけに　■make one's escape 首尾
よく逃げる、まんまと逃げおおせる　■get into trouble 面倒を起こす　■uneasy 形 不安
な、心配な　■arrest 動 ～を逮捕する　■any moment 今にも

を知っているかと聞いたところ、「シカゴで一番危険な犯罪者」との返事がきました。この返信が届いたちょうどその夜、ヒルトン・キュービット氏がスレイニーからの最後の踊る人形たちの絵を送ってきたのです。判明した文字をあてはめると、このようになります。

ELSIE . RE . ARE TO MEET THY GO .

　ここに2つのPと1つのDを加えて伝言を完成させてみると、メッセージの内容が、以前の会いたいという懇願から危険を匂わすものへと変わってきたことがわかりました。ELSIE, PREPARE TO MEET THY GOD.（エルシー、神に会う覚悟をせよ）　すぐさま私は、ワトソンとともにノーフォークへと駆けつけましたが、残念なことに、事件を食い止めるには遅すぎました」

　「あなたとこの事件に取り組むことができて光栄です」とマーティン警部は心を込めて言った。「ただ、一言言わせていただけますか。あなたはご自身で説明できればそれでいいのでしょうけれども、私はそうはいきません。そのエルリッジに滞在しているエイブ・スレイニーなる男が本当に犯人だったとして、私がここにいる間に逃げられていたら、私としては大変困ったことになるのです」

　「ご心配には及びません。逃げようなどとはしませんよ」

　「なぜおわかりなのですか」

　「逃げようとすることは、自分が犯人だと公言することになるからです」

　「それなら逮捕しに行きましょう」

　「まもなくここへ来るはずですよ」

"But why should he come?"

"Because I have written and asked him."

"But this is unbelievable, Mr. Holmes! Why should he come because you asked him? Would not such a thing make him more careful, or even make him fly?"

"I think I have known how to write the letter in such a way to ensure he comes," said Sherlock Holmes. "In fact I am sure that this is the gentleman himself coming up the drive."

A man was walking up the path which led to the door. He was a tall, good-looking fellow with a big hat. He came up the path as if the place belonged to him, and we heard him ring at the door.

"I think, gentlemen," said Holmes, quietly, "that we had best take up our positions behind the door. Every care must be taken when dealing with such a man. You will need your handcuffs, Inspector Martin. You can leave the talking to me."

We waited quietly for a minute, one of those minutes that one never forgets. Then the door opened and the man stepped in. In a moment Holmes put a gun to his head, and Inspector Martin put the handcuffs over his hands. It was all done so quickly that the fellow was helpless before he knew what had happened. He looked from one to the other with a pair of angry eyes. Then he burst into a strange laugh.

■unbelievable 形 信じられない ■make 動 (人) に〜させる ■fly 動 (人が) 急いで逃げる ■in such a way to そのような方法で ■ensure 動 〜を確かにする ■come up 立ち寄る ■drive 名 (通りから家までの) アプローチ ■good-looking 形 顔立ちの

256

「なぜ彼がここへ?」

「彼に手紙を書き、そう頼んだからです」

「そんな、信じられませんよ、ホームズさん。奴が来いと言われたから来るだなんて。そんなことをしたら警戒させてしまうか、逃げかねませんよ」

「僕は、彼が間違いなくここへ来るような手紙の書き方を知っているつもりですから」とシャーロック・ホームズは言った。「間違いなさそうです。その紳士がこちらへ向かっておいでです」

一人の男が玄関へ続く道を歩いてくる。背が高く、整った顔立ちをしていて、つば広の帽子を被っていた。まるでこの場所は自分の領地だとでもいうような素ぶりで小道を歩き、呼び鈴を鳴らした。

「諸君」とホームズが声をひそめて言った、「我々はドアの後ろに隠れた方がよさそうですね。あの手の男を相手にするには、できる限りの用心をしなくてはなりません。警部、手錠も必要です。話をするのは僕に任せて」

私たちは1分間ほど、息をひそめて待った。一生忘れることがない1分だ。やがて扉が開き、男が入ってきた。と、次の瞬間、ホームズが拳銃を男の頭に突きつけ、マーティン警部が手錠をはめた。すべてがあっという間に行われたので、男は抵抗もできないでいた。そして自分に起こった事態をようやく把握してから、憎しみのこもった目で私たちをひとりひとり睨みつけ、妙な笑い声をあげた。

良い ■fellow 图 男 ■take up one's positions 配置に就く ■handcuff 图 手錠 ■helpless 形 自分ではどうすることもできない ■look from one to the other with 〜 で代わる代わる見る ■pair of 一対の〜

"Well, gentlemen, you have the drop on me this time. But I came here in answer to a letter from Mrs. Hilton Cubitt. Don't tell me that she helped you to catch me."

"Mrs. Hilton Cubitt was gravely wounded, and is at death's door."

The man gave a cry which rang through the house.

"You're mad!" he cried. "It was he that was hurt, not she. Who would have hurt little Elsie? I may have seemed dangerous to her—God help me—but I would never have touched a hair of her pretty head."

"She was found, badly wounded, by the side of her dead husband."

He fell with a cry to the seat, and put his face in his hands. For a few minutes he was quiet. Then he raised his face once more and seemed sad but in control.

"I have nothing to hide from you, gentlemen," said he. "If I shot the man it was because he shot at me, and there's no murder in that. But if you think that I could hurt that woman, then you don't know either me or her. I tell you, there is no man in this world who loved a woman more than I loved her. She was promised to me years ago. Who was this Englishman that he should come between us? I tell you that I had the first right to her, and that I was only trying to get what was mine."

■have the drop on（人）の機先を制する、（人）を出し抜く ■at death's door 瀕死の状態で ■ring 動（大きな音が）響き渡る ■seem 動 ～のように見える ■by the side of ～のそばに ■raise 動（顔を）上げる ■in control 抑制して ■hide 動 隠す ■there's no murder in that そこに殺人はない ■come between ～の間に入る ■first right 優先権

「なるほど、俺をはめたわけだな。だが、俺はヒルトン・キュービット夫人の手紙に応じてここに来たんだ。あいつが俺を捕まえる手助けをしたなんてことはないんだろう?」
「ヒルトン・キュービット夫人は重体で、危篤状態だ」

男は叫び声をあげた。その声は家じゅうに轟いた。
「ふざけるな。俺が撃ったのは男のほうで、あいつじゃない。一体だれが愛しいエルシーを撃ったんだ。怖い思いをさせたかもしれないが——神様に誓ってもいい——髪の毛一本たりとも触っていない」

「夫人は、ひどい傷を負った状態で発見された。亡くなった夫のそばで」

男はうめき声を上げて椅子に倒れこみ、両手で顔を覆った。ほんのしばらく静かにしていたが、また顔をあげた。動揺してはいたが、落ち着きはとり戻しているようだった。
「隠すことは何もない」と男は話し始めた。「俺が男を撃ったなら、それはやつが俺を撃ったからなんだ。殺そうとしたわけじゃない。でも、あんたたちが、俺がエルシーを傷つけたと思ってるなら、俺のこともあいつのこともわかっていないんだ。いいか、俺はあいつを愛していた。この世界のどんな男がどんな女を愛するよりも激しく愛していた。何年も前にあいつは、俺のものになると約束してくれたんだ。あのイギリス人が割り込んできたんだよ。いいか、俺には彼女に対する優先権がある。自分のものを手に入れようとしただけだ」

"She broke away from you when she found out what you were really like," said Holmes. "She left America to get away from you, and she married an honorable gentleman in England. You followed her and made problems for her in her new life. You have brought about the death of a good man and driven his wife to attempted suicide. That is your record in this business Mr. Abe Slaney, and you will answer for it to the law."

"If Elsie dies, I care nothing of what becomes of me," said the American. He opened one of his hands and held out a piece of paper. "Look here," he cried with a look of hope in his eyes, "you're not trying to fool me over this, are you? If the lady is as badly hurt as you say, who was it that wrote this note?"

"I wrote it to bring you here."

"You wrote it? There was no one on earth outside our group who knew the secret of the dancing men. How came you to write it?"

"What one man can make up another one can figure out," said Holmes. "There is a cab coming to take you to Norwich, Mr. Slaney. But, meanwhile, you have time to make good some of the trouble you have caused. Do you know that the police thought that Mrs. Hilton Cubitt murdered her husband, and that it was only because of what I know, that they haven't investigated her? The least that you can do is to make it clear to the whole world that she played no part, directly or indirectly, in his sad end."

■break away from ～と決別する　■get away from ～から離れる　■honorable 形 立派な　■bring about ～を引き起こす　■drive someone to（人）を～させる　■attempted suicide 自殺未遂者［行為］　■hold out ～を差し出す　■with a look of hope 期待の表情で　■over 前 ～に関して　■how come どうして、なぜ

「夫人が君から離れたのは、君の本性に気付いたからだよ」とホームズは言った。「彼女はアメリカから逃げ出して、イギリスで、立派な男性と結婚した。君は彼女を追いかけ、彼女の新しい生活の邪魔をした。そしてひとりの善良な男に死をもたらし、その妻を自殺に追いやった。エイブ・スレイニー、以上がこの件について君がやってきたことだ。法の裁きを受けたまえ」

「エルシーが死ぬなら、自分もどうなったっていいんだ」と彼が言った。そして片方の手を開き、紙切れを突き出した。「これを見てくれよ」。彼は叫んだ。その目は、まだ希望を捨てていないと語っていた。「俺をだますつもりじゃないだろうな。あんたたちの言うとおりにあいつが重傷だというなら、だれがこれを書いたというんだ?」

「僕が描いた。君をここにおびきよせるために」

「あんたが? この踊る人形の秘密を知っているのは、俺たち一味以外にはいないはずだ。どうやってこれを描いた?」

「人が作ったものならば、誰かが解くことができるものさ」とホームズは言った。「スレイニーさん、君をノリッジへ運ぶ馬車がこちらに向かっている。しかし、君が引き起こした悲劇に対して、多少の罪滅ぼしをする時間がある。いいか、警察は、ヒルトン・キュービット夫人が夫を殺したと考えていたんだよ。夫人が告発されなかったのは、私が持ちあわせていた情報があったから、ただそれだけだ。君ができる最後のことは、彼女が夫の悲しい死に対して直接的にも間接的にも責任がないということを、全世界に明らかにすることだ」

■make up 作り出す、考え出す　■figure out 解明する　■make good（約束・義務など）を）果たす　■least 図 最小のもの　■make clear はっきりさせる　■play a part ～に関与する　■directly or indirectly 直接間接を問わず

"I ask nothing better," said the American. "I guess the very best case I can make for myself is to say what truly happened."

"It is necessary for me to tell you that it will be taken down in writing, and may be used in evidence against you," cried Inspector Martin, with the wonderful fair play of British criminal law.

Slaney was unmoved.

"I'll chance that," said he. "First of all, I want you gentlemen to understand that I have known this lady since she was a child. There were seven of us in a group in Chicago, and her father was the chief of it. He was a clever man, was old Patrick. It was he who made up that writing, which would pass as a child's picture unless you happened to have the key to it. Well, Elsie learned some of our ways, but she couldn't stand the business. She had some lawful money of her own, so she ran away to London. She had been promised to me, and she would have married me, I believe, if I had given up my life of crime, but she would have nothing to do with anything against the law. It was only after her marriage to this Englishman that I was able to find out where she was. I wrote to her, but got no answer. After that I came over, and, as letters were of no use, I put my notes where she could read them.

■ask nothing better 望むところだ　■very best case 最善の展開　■truly 副 本当に　■take down 記録する、書き留める　■fair play 公正な取り扱い　■unmoved 形 心を動かされない　■chance 動 いちかばちかやってみる　■chief 名 (組織の) 長　■old 形 親しい～、親愛なる～　■happen to たまたま～する　■key 名 鍵　■can't stand ～には我慢ならない　■lawful 形 合法の　■of one's own 自分自身の　■of no use 用をなさない

　「望むところだ」と、そのアメリカ人は言った。「俺にできる最善のことは、真実を話すことなんだろう」

　「ひとつ言っておかなくてはならないのだが、君が話したことは書面に残される。君に不利な証拠として使われることもあるだろう」と警部が口を添えた。大英帝国刑法の素晴らしき公正の精神である。

　スレイニーの気持ちは変わらなかった。

　「了解した」と彼は語り始めた。「まずあんたたちにわかってほしいのは、俺とあいつは、幼馴染だったっていうことだ。俺たち7人はシカゴの悪党団で、エルシーの父親は一味のボスだった。頭のきれる男だったよ。パトリックのおやじと呼ばれていた。この暗号を考え出したのもおやじだよ。ふつうなら子供の落書きとして片づけられるところだろう。あんたはたまたまその鍵を手に入れたけれどね。それで、エルシーは一味のやっていることに気付いたんだが、その仕事に耐えられず、自分で合法的に金を作って、ロンドンへと逃げたんだ。その前に俺とは結婚の約束をしていたんだよ。俺が足を洗っていたなら、結婚してくれていたと思う。あいつは法に背くことには関わりあいたくなかったんだろう。俺がエルシーの居所を突き止めたときには、あのイギリス人と結婚した後だった。手紙を出したけれども、返事はこない。手紙じゃ役にたたないから、こっちにやってきて、あいつの目につく場所に伝言を描いたんだ。

"Well, I have been here a month now. I lived in that farm, where I had a room down below, and could get in and out every night, without anyone knowing. I tried all I could to get Elsie to come away with me. I knew that she read the notes, for once she wrote an answer under one of them. Then my anger got the better of me, and I tried to make her afraid. She sent me a letter then, asking me to go away, and saying that it would break her heart if anything should happen to destroy her husband's name. She said that she would come down when her husband was asleep at three in the morning, and speak with me through the end window, if I would go away afterwards and leave her in peace. She came down and brought money with her, trying to pay me to go. This made me mad, and I caught her arm and tried to pull her through the window. At that moment her husband rushed in with a gun in his hand. Elsie had fallen to the floor, and we were face to face. I had my gun also, and I held it up to show him, still hoping to get away. He fired and missed me. I shot almost at the same moment, and down he dropped. I made away across the garden, and as I went I heard the window shut behind me. They are true words, gentlemen, and I heard no more about it until that lad came riding up with a note which made me come round here and give myself into your hands."

■a room down below 地下の一室　■get in and out 出入りする　■come away with ～と一緒に去る　■for once 一度だけ　■get the better of ～をしのぐ　■make someone afraid （人）をおじけづさせる　■go away 立ち去る

264

　そうだな、ここに来て1ヵ月になるよ。あの農場に滞在して、地下室で暮らしていたよ。夜ならいつでも、誰にも気づかれずに出入りできた。エルシーが自分と逃げてくれるのならと、できる限りのことをした。俺の伝言は読んでくれているようだった。一度、俺が描いた伝言の下に、返事をくれたからね。俺は怒りのあまり我を忘れてしまって、あいつを脅そうとした。するとあいつは手紙をよこした。俺にここから立ち去るようにと頼んできたんだ。夫の名誉に傷がつくようなことが起こるかと思うと心配で心がはりさけそうだというんだ。あいつは、朝の3時、夫が眠っているときに抜け出して、窓ごしに俺と話をするから、それきり立ち去ってくれ、そっとしておいてくれ、と言ってきた。あいつはやってきたよ。金を持ってきて、その金で俺を追い払おうとしたんだ。俺はかっとなって、あいつの腕をつかみ、窓から引きずり下ろそうとした。その時、あいつの旦那が銃を手に走ってきた。エルシーは床に倒れ、俺は奴と向き合った。俺も銃を取り出した。奴を威嚇して逃げるつもりだった。あいつが撃ってきたが、弾は逸れた。俺も同時に撃って、奴は倒れた。俺は庭を横切って逃げたけれど、後ろで窓が閉まる音が聞こえた。これが真実だ。その後はあの少年が手紙を持ってきて、俺はのこのことここへやってきて、手錠をかけられた、それが全てだよ」

■break one's heart （人）を悲嘆に暮れさせる　■end window 妻窓《建物の妻側（短手方向）に設置された窓》　■face to face 向かい合って　■hold it up 持ち上げる　■make away 急いで去る　■lad 图 少年　■ride up 乗りつける

A cab had driven up while the American had been talking. Two policemen sat inside. Inspector Martin rose and touched his prisoner on the shoulder.

"It is time for us to go."

"Can I see her first?"

"No, she has not come round. Mr. Sherlock Holmes, I only hope that, if ever again I have an important case, I shall be able to have you by my side."

We stood at the window and watched the cab drive away. As I turned back my eye caught the piece of paper which Abe Slaney had left on the table. It was the note that had fooled him into coming.

"See if you can read it, Watson," said he, with a smile.

It contained no word, but this little line of dancing men:

"If you use the key which I have explained," said Holmes, "you will find that it simply says, 'Come here at once.' I was sure that he would do it, since he would think that it could only be from the lady. And so, my dear Watson, we have ended by turning the dancing men to good when they have so often been used for bad, and I think that I have kept my promise of giving you something unusual for your notebook. Three-forty is our train, and I think we should be back in Baker Street for dinner."

■cab 图 馬車　■drive up（車で）やって来る　■prisoner 图 拘束された人　■come round 意識を回復する　■by one's side ～のそばに、身近に　■drive away（車で）走り去る　■fool someone into（人）をだまして～させる　■see if ～かどうかを見る　■turn ～ to good ～を善に変える

アメリカ人が話している間に、馬車が到着していた。中には2人の警察官がいた。マーティン警部は立ち上がり、犯人の肩に手をかけた。

「さあ、行こう」

「あいつにひと目会えませんか」

「だめだ。意識が戻っていないんだよ。シャーロック・ホームズさん、今後また大きな事件があったときには、ぜひともご一緒できたらと願っております」

私たちは窓際に立ち、馬車が去っていくのを見ていた。私が振り返ると、スレイニーが机の上に置いていった紙切れが目にとまった。彼をここへおびき寄せた手紙だ。

「それが読めるかね、ワトソン君」とホームズが微笑みながら言った。

そこには文字はなく、踊る人形がいくつか並んでいるだけだった。

「僕が説明した解読の鍵を使えばわかるだろう。『Come here at once』（すぐに来て）と書いてあるだけさ。奴は、あの夫人からに違いないと思うだろうから、絶対に来るだろうと思っていた。そうだ、ワトソンくん、この踊る人形はずいぶんと悪いことに使われてきたけれど、最後にはいいことに使われたんだよ。そして僕は、君の事件簿の中に珍しい事件を加えるという約束を果たせた。3時40分の列車に乗ろう。そうすれば、ベーカー街に戻って夕食を食べることができる」

To finish the story, Abe Slaney was not killed for murder, but was given life in prison in consideration of the fact that Hilton Cubitt had fired the first shot. Of Mrs. Hilton Cubitt, I have heard that she recovered completely, and that she has not remarried, and she spends her whole life caring for the poor and looking after her husband's home and workers.

■life in prison 終身刑　■in consideration of ～を考慮 [斟酌] して　■of 前 について

　最後に付け加えておこう。エイブ・スレイニーは、ヒルトン・キュービット氏が先に撃ったという事実を考慮され、死刑は免れたが終身刑とされた。ヒルトン・キュービット夫人については、その後完全に回復したとのことだが、再婚はせず、余生を慈善事業に捧げ、愛する夫の家と使用人たちの生活を守っているという。

覚えておきたい英語表現

> **That is why I must get to the bottom of this matter.**
> （p.198, 7行目）
>
> ですから、私はこの件を徹底的に調べなくてはと思ったのです。

【解説】get to the bottom of this matterは、「この事柄の、本質・真相をつきとめる」という意味です。

【例文】① Let's get to the bottom of this incident.
この事件の真相に迫ろうではないか。

② This is a matter of urgency.
緊急な事態だ。

> **I'm not much of a storyteller.** （p.200, 1行目）
>
> 私は話すのは得意ではないので。

【解説】not much of 〜 は、「〜があまりうまくない」という意味です。
storytellerは、「物語の語り手」のことです。 物語を語るということを、storytelling
と言います。物語とは言っても、童話やフィクションのみならず、身の上話や、見聞
きしたり、体験した事柄を語ることも指します。
人は、興味深い物語や、うまい語り手のお話に惹きつけられます。優れた指導者は、
great storyteller（素晴らしい語り手）の人が多いです。

【例文】① I'm not much of a singer, but I love to sing.
私は歌がうまいとはいえませんが、歌うことは大好きです。

② Barack Obama is a great storyteller and his stories resonate among
people of all streams of life.
オバマ大統領は偉大な語り手で、彼が語る物語は、多種多様な人々の心に響く。

> **I should be proud to think that we were acting together.**
> （p.226, 6行目）
>
> 御一緒させていただければ光栄です。

【解説】I should be proud to ～ は、「～することを誇りに思うべき」という意味です。to think we were acting togetherは、「（ホームズと）協力したと思えることを、誇らしく思う」で、ホームズへの敬意を表しています。

【例文】① I should be most proud to work with you.
　　　　あなたと協働できることを非常に誇りに思います。

　　　② You should be proud of your son.
　　　　立派な息子さんですね。
　　　　＊「息子さんを誇りに思うべきです」という意味の、褒め言葉です。

> **I believe that it was undoubtedly so.** （p.238, 下から4行目）
>
> 僕はそうに違いないとにらんでいるんですがね。

【解説】I believe は、「～と確信している」という意味です。日本人は自分の考えを述べるときによく、「～だと思います」という表現を使いますが、英語では、"I think" を連発すると、自分の発言に自信が持てない人のような印象を与えます。確信していることを述べるときには、"I believe ～"、"I am convinced that ～"、"I am confident of/that ～" などの表現を使いましょう。
undoubtedlyは、「疑う余地もなく」という意味です。「絶対にそうだ」と断定する時に使えます。

【例文】① I believe in our success.
　　　　成功すると確信しています。

　　　② Undoubtedly, our alliance will lead to a global business expansion.
　　　　我々の提携が、事業の世界的な拡張につながることは明らかだ。

English Conversational Ability Test
国際英語会話能力検定

● E-CATとは…
英語が話せるようになるための
テストです。インターネット
ベースで、30分であなたの発
話力をチェックします。

www.ecatexam.com

● iTEP®とは…
世界各国の企業、政府機関、アメリカの大学
300校以上が、英語能力判定テストとして採用。
オンラインによる90分のテストで文法、リー
ディング、リスニング、ライティング、スピー
キングの5技能をスコア化。iTEP®は、留学、就
職、海外赴任などに必要な、世界に通用する英
語力を総合的に評価する画期的なテストです。

www.itepexamjapan.com

[IBC 対訳ライブラリー]

英語で読むシャーロック・ホームズ [新版]

2013年 1 月 6 日　初版第 1 刷発行
2021年 3 月22日　　　第 7 刷発行
2023年 5 月 4 日　新版第 1 刷発行
2024年 8 月 8 日　　　第 2 刷発行

原 著 者　コナン・ドイル
翻訳・解説　井上 久美

発行者　賀 川　洋

発行所　**IBCパブリッシング株式会社**
　　　　〒162-0804 東京都新宿区中里町29番3号 菱秀神楽坂ビル
　　　　Tel. 03-3513-4511　Fax. 03-3513-4512
　　　　www.ibcpub.co.jp

印刷所　　株式会社シナノパブリッシングプレス

© IBC Publishing. Inc. 2023

Printed in Japan

ISBN978-4-7946-0758-4